Dec 01

To Tom Full[...]
This B[...] ft From
Our Mutual Friend Johnny Z, A
Supporter of Our Western Heritage
& The American Cowboy —
Best Wishes

Collector's limited edition

2,000 numbered registered copies

This copy is number _____0281_____

Cowboy Poetry

Rhymes, Reasons and Pack Saddle Proverbs
by Chris Isaacs

Foreword by
Larry McWhorter

Edited by Janice Coggin

Cowboy Miner PRODUCTIONS

Cowboy Poetry, Rhymes, Reasons and Pack Saddle Proverbs by Chris Isaacs
Copyright © 2001 Chris Isaacs
Illustration, "The Packer," on page 13 Copyright © 2001 Jim Ford
Edited by Janice Coggin

Publisher:
  Cowboy Miner Productions
  P.O. Box 9674
  Phoenix, AZ 85068
  Phone: (602) 944-3763
  www.CowboyMiner.com

Publisher's Cataloging-in-Publication Data

Isaacs, Chris 1944–
Cowboy Poetry : Rhymes, Reasons and Pack Saddle Proverbs by Chris
  Isaacs / Chris Isaacs. Edited by Janice Coggin. Foreword by Larry
  McWhorter.
  p. cm.

  ISBN: 0-9662091-6-8

1. Cowboy—Poetry. 2. Ranch life—Poetry. 3. West (U.S.)—Poetry
  I. Title
Library of Congress Catalog Card Number: 2001092358

Book Design & Typesetting: SageBrush Publications, Tempe, Arizona
Jacket Design: ATG Productions, Christy A. Moeller, Phoenix, Arizona
Printing: Bang Printing, Brainerd, Minnesota
Printed and bound in the United States of America

Dedication

This book is dedicated with love to my wife, Helen, and to our children, Sis, Bud, Artie, Leesee, and Max, who have ridden the trails, prowled the pastures, and stood on the stages with me; and also to Shane-O, who, God willing, someday will do the same.

Contents

4

Foreword

I've heard it has been said in some circles of intelligentsia that rhymed and metered poetry is not poetry at all, but merely an "exercise in frivolous, lyrical acrobatics" where meaning is sacrificed to accommodate a restrictive rhyme scheme. To most of these critics the problem is compounded if the writer happens to have a little "bow" to his/her legs. Or is a (gasp) "cowboy poet."

To these learned detractors of traditional stylings I have but one response: At least you don't need hallucinogenics before or after the consumption of our craft in order to "get it." You don't need to be depressed, oppressed, suicidal, or angry in order to express yourself. You don't even need a two-hundred-dollar-an-hour shrink to ask how you "feel" about things.

If you enjoy traditional verse, cowboy or otherwise, then you are probably pretty secure within yourself. You have no need of further complicating your life by trying to discern the erratic rantings of some sociopath who has decided life is unfair. No, you probably just want to enjoy yourself by reading something you can understand, written by someone who has lived life as he/she has found it. Taking the bitter with the sweet, knowing neither lasts forever and tomorrow is a brand new day full of hope or disappointment. Either way, life marches on and you're part of the parade, so grab your baton and twirl.

Folks, meet Chris Isaacs.

Chris's view of the cowboy life can be seen from so many different angles because he has lived so many aspects of it. Chris can ride the bull, drive the bull, pack the bull, and he can shoot the bull with the best of them.

What people like about Chris, and others like him, is that he never sees himself as the hero or the put-upon, but rather as one of the blessed few who has had the opportunity to make his living doing the things he loves to do. The things we write about are merely a loving recollection of paths we'll never ride again and the lessons and philosophies we've picked up along the way that make us who we are today.

I once had a lady ask me what it was about our craft that held such an appeal for people. I told her I didn't know. We basically write our verse for ourselves and each other and just welcome other folks to come along for the ride.

What we write of is not just about horses, cattle, and elements; it's more about the bonds we've forged through common experience with people we may never get to meet. It's something you can't fake or concoct.

A cowboy can tell pretty quickly if the author has "been there" or not just by the way he phrases things. There is something about being a part of a certain class that allows one to recognize another of his ilk sometimes at a mere glance.

This kinship is something so rare in today's fast-paced world that those who truly are part of a clan are jealous of the place they hold because of what they've gone through to get there. They had to earn the right to be there and see it as a sacred trust to be guarded and to be presented to the world with reverence and respect to those who rode before.

You don't just buy a saddle and become a cowboy any more than you buy a scalpel and become a surgeon. And you certainly can't write about it with any authority. It may be entertaining, but it won't hold water with those in the know.

One such interloper once told me he liked to write "this cowboy stuff" but that he wrote "real" poetry, too. I wasn't very diplomatic in letting him know that what we wrote was just as legitimate American literature as anything anyone else has written. Whether it's the *Midnight Ride of Paul Revere* or *When the Work's All Done This Fall*, the story of an American experience is being related.

These are the kinds of things you will find in the following pages. Chris captures the flavor of America as his paths have revealed her to him. The animals he writes of are more than mere beasts of burden. They are more like co-workers to be respected and, in some cases, honored adversaries that made him find the best in himself.

The land he writes of Chris sees as the gift God intended it to be. He knows as a steward of that gift that the land is to be used for food production, shelter and proof of God's existence. It is not to be shelved as a museum piece and rendered useless and overprotected as some would have us do. He knows the land is best served when it is serving.

The old bunkhouse he tells of reminds us there are faces to our past and they need to be remembered.

And then there are the poems of people God has put in his life. Family and friends are truly gifts Chris holds dear, just as those who know Chris hold him dear. Chris loves God, his family, his friends, his country, and his way of life in a way we all should, honestly and unashamedly.

And, folks, being honest doesn't always mean you have to tear something down or cuss it. The good in this world is just as real as the bad. Chris chooses to focus on the former and lives and writes that way. And what's wrong with that?

Larry McWhorter
Weatherford, Texas

Acknowledgments

I don't consider myself a "Poet," I think of myself as more of a "Rhymer." I have, however, been fortunate enough to have some great performers and writers of poetry in my circle of friends, people like Joel, Ross, Jesse, Randy, Kent, Waddie, Leon, Dennis, Wallace, J. B., Sunny, Buck, and Larry. If you are a true fan of Cowboy Poetry, the last names aren't needed; you know who I'm talking about. I owe a great deal of thanks to these friends; they make me want to work harder at my craft!

I owe so much to so many: Helen, my wife of thirty-four years, who has stood by me through the good times and the bad. My mother, who is always there for me no matter what. My dad, who taught me the value of work and how to laugh at life. My kids, who have driven me nuts at times, but who have never made me hang my head in shame. No one could ask more. I love you all!

Thanks also to my high school English teacher, Mr. Jay Dean Jones, whom I have not told that I've written a book for fear that piece of information might cause him to have a stroke.

To Curt Brummett for taking a rhymer, who wrote the same way that he talked, and finally helping him to understand what poor ol' Mr. Jones had been trying to explain to him thirty years earlier.

To every cowboy that I have ever had the opportunity to work around and especially those who took the time to "show me!"

To the ever-growing circle of cowboy performers who are passing on a tradition that is also a valuable look at a true American icon.

To the cowboy poetry fans out there who are becoming more and more informed and discriminating.

To Larry McWhorter for writing the foreword. You're a damn fine bench mark, pard!

A special thanks to Janice Coggin for taking on this particular project.

And to my Father in Heaven for allowing me the privilege!

Introduction

I have often been asked the question, "Where did you get the idea for that poem?" So with that thought in mind I decided to put together "Rhymes and Reasons." Some of my poems are obviously written from old jokes I've heard someone tell, and I'm not sure where the ideas came from for some of them. I have written down some of the more interesting reasons for a few of my poems to try to answer some of your questions.

Cowboys, as a rule, have a fairly colorful language, and the Packsaddle Proverbs are just a collection of sayings that I have gathered over the years. Most all of them are from other folks (I ain't had too many original ideas in my life) so you have probably heard a good share of them at sometime or other.

It is my heartfelt hope that you will enjoy the journey that is ours to take together through the pages of this book. You aren't going to find any wild stampedes on a stormy night or shootouts at high noon. Those stories have been done many times and certainly done better than I could do them. What you will find, hopefully, is a look at "life" from an old cowboy/packer's point of view. I hope that these poems and thoughts will make you smile, laugh, cry, ponder, remember, or imagine. Hopefully, through my eyes you will recognize some person or place you have known, or maybe meet some new folks, or go someplace that you have never been before. If I can touch your imagination for a brief moment with just one or two of these poems then I am pleased beyond measure.

I take full responsibility for the contents of this book, be they good or bad (I couldn't find anyone else who would accept any of the blame), but without the help of lots of people it would never have happened. Thanks for the stories, ideas, and encouragement.

So, friends, I hope you enjoy the ride. Remember to check your back trail once in a while to make sure they're still comin', and as my ol' pard Buck would have said, "Keep out of the wire."

Chris Isaacs
Eagar, Arizona

The Cowboy Creation

Here's to all the "real cowboys"
 (May God preserve the breed)
 Who make their living horseback
 And still live proud and free.

Who ride the "grande pastures"
 Or the feedlot alleyways.
 Who fight the heat of summer
 And those freezing winter days.

Who wouldn't trade their worn-out "kack"
 For the trappings of a king.
 Who still believe in God and Country
 And the joy that family brings.

Men who still believe that freedom
 Is the most important thing in life.
 That you treat a lady with respect
 Be she a stranger or your wife.

Who use a different way to score
 The tally book of success.
 Who keep the company of horse and cow
 And avoid the cities' urban mess.

Success they measure by the ruler
 Of honesty and truth,
 Though their manner may be bashful
 And their style a bit uncouth.

Their ways have stood the test of time.
They wear well the cowboy pedigree.
And these reluctant heroes of the west
Have created ten million "wanna-be's."

The American Cowboy is the only true icon that this country has ever produced. He has become a symbol of America throughout the world. As a packer and wrangler I have had the opportunity to deal with people from all over the world, and it has always amazed me that folks from foreign countries still come to the west expecting to find "guntoting cowboys and Indians" here in Arizona. They are fascinated by the west and anything "cowboy." Hollywood has had a lot to do with this phenomenon, but I think the real cowboys are still mystified by the fact that they are viewed as a "symbol." They shouldn't be surprised. The values that most of them hold dear are the values that made this country great to begin with. Love of family, faith in God, a strong belief in right and wrong, a love of country, a strong work ethic, a handshake worth more than a contract, these values are admirable in any society. Not a bad type of "symbol" to be.

The Proposition

He rode into our spring camp
  On a tall blood-colored bay.
  We were pushed up to the campfire,
  The branding finished for the day.

  He took an offered cup of coffee
  And ask which one of us was boss?
  Clark Hunt looked up from his tally book
  And said, "That'd be me ol' Hoss."

  The stranger shook Clark's rope-burned hand
  And with a steady gaze
  Said, "I was hoping you could use me
  At your branding a few days."

  Clark looked the stranger up and down,
  Then said as he dipped up some "snoose,"
  "I don't guess that I need you, Pard.
  I've got all the good hands I can use."

  Well, the stranger broke a little smile
  And with a twinkle in his eye
  Said, "You're passing up a right top hand;
  You ought to give me just a try.

  You'll find hiring me's a bargain, sir.
  There's damn little I can't do.
  In fact, I'll guarantee beyond a doubt
  I'll be the top hand on this crew."

Well, this speech made ol' Clark bristle,
'Cause he was right proud of this mob.
He said, "That talk is mighty bold
For a man who's looking for a job."

Well, the stranger spit into the fire
And squatted down at a leisure position.
He tipped his hat back on his head,
And made this astounding proposition.

"Now, Mr. Hunt, I'm a right top hand,
So I'll tell you what I'll do.
I'll outride, outrope, or whip in a fight
Any three men on your crew.

"And for our little contest,
There should be a prize, of course.
So, if I win, I get the job.
If I lose, you get my horse."

Well, ol' Clark was plumb astonished
At the stranger's talk so bold.
But, as a betting man himself,
He knew 'twas time to call or fold.

He said, "You've got a bet, sir,
And you'll live to rue this day,
While you're riding shank's mare down the road
And I'm sitting on your bay."

So Clark Hunt picked his men with care,
And each knew his job well.
'Cause little Jim Hanes, ol' Clark was sure,
Could ride any horse this side of hell.

And Curly Bob was as handy with a rope
As anyone Clark had ever found.
But his ace in the hole was T-bone Jones,
Who'd whipped every tough for miles around.

Clark picked out two outlaw broncs,
And both boys screwed down their kacks.*
And though Jim's spurs caused the hair to fly,
The stranger's ride made Jim look like a hack.

Then Curly Bob roped a brindle steer
And tripped him with his twine,
But the stranger tripped and tied his down
In roughly half the time.

Clark said, "OK, T-bone, get warmed up,
'Cause with this feller I'm through messin'.
Show no mercy on him, son.
You teach this boy a lesson."

Ol' T-bone met Clark's steady gaze
And said, "Boss, I've watched him well
To see just what mistakes he makes,
And when there's a weakness, I can tell.

"'Cause, I don't want to make the mistakes
We seen made by Jim and Bob,
And Boss, I've come up with a damn good plan.
Let's give this guy the job!"

*Kack – Saddle

Ol' Bob and Clark Hunt, 1925

Clark Hunt was a good friend and the closest thing to a grandfather that I had growing up. He was a neighbor of mine for several years, and our friendship was rock solid. He was a great influence in my life in many ways, but one of the things that I most remember about him was his storytelling ability. I've often thought how much he would have enjoyed the cowboy poetry gatherings that are now so popular. He would have fit right in.

As a young man he ran with one of Arizona's famous old cowboys, Breezy Cox, and had some great stories from that time in his life. My poem, "THE PROPOSITION," is based on a story he told me about Breezy. I used Clark as one of the characters in that poem. I hope it would have pleased him.

19

Antiques

It was just an old stirrup that I found in a box,
All covered with weeds and grass.
An "old-timey" oxbow, all tattered and worn,
Just a relic of the past.

I started to toss it back inside
And go upon my way,
But then thought, If this antique could talk,
I wonder what it would say?

Did it hang on the side of a gentle ol' hoss
Bought for the grandkids to ride?
Or did it swing fore and aft on a salty young bronc
As some "hand" spurred the hair off his hide?

Did it help ease the strain in the small of a back
On a long trot one early morn?
Or maybe help take the jerk when some young "ranahan"*
Stuck a loop on an ol' mossy horn?

Did it serve as a handle for some "little button"
Tryin' to climb up an ol' hoss's side?
Or hold the fresh-polished boots of a young buckaroo
When courtin' his future bride?

Oh, the things we could learn from them 'ol "antiques"
If only they could tell;
We'd gain wisdom and knowledge and other such gifts.
Things that would serve us so well.

*Ranahan – someone who is "wild and wooley."

But then I thought to myself, This stirrup can't talk.
It's got no tales to be told.
Then my "mind's eye" saw friends I'd known all my life
Who now are growin' old.

And I made silent resolve to take the time
And visit my older friends,
To ask about old times and days
And try to make amends

For treating them like that stirrup
Just because they're gettin' old.
'Cause if we just take the time to listen
They've got stories to be told.

It's the "antiques" who have been down life's trail
Who' like to give us a hand,
If we'll just take a while to visit old folks,
And try to listen and understand.

21

Like so many of my poems, when I come up with an idea, and then start to write, they sometimes take off on their own in a direction far removed from what I originally had in mind. "Antiques" is a prime example of that. We were shipping cattle one fall for Ellis Wiltbank on the Double Lazy Y, when I found a beat-up old-timey oxbow stirrup in a pile of junk. I threw it in the truck, and back home I got to wondering what stories it could tell if it could talk. I started the poem with that in mind; but the farther along the poem got, the more I started thinking about the older folks that I have known and the rich stories that they have shared with me. We owe so much to the older generations who went through so much and have so much to share. May God grant us the prudence to listen.

 A good story is like a fine wine, it usually gets better with age!

The Journey

Just a kid, that's all I was, still wet behind the ears.
He'd been top hand on that place then for many years.
He took me underneath his wing and helped me make a hand;
Taught me things that I should know when riding for the brand.
To always give the best I had whatever the job demanded.
That if you look you'll find an ace in any cards you're handed.

He'd say, "Whatever trail you travel, kid,
And whatever life may bring,
Just be thankful that you're riding,
'Cause *the journey* is the thing."

We rode the Arizona desert and New Mexico's long plain.
Fought the heat out in west Texas and Oklahoma's driving rain.
Montana held us for a season with its wide and open sky;
Whichever way the wind blew, these two tumbleweeds would try.
I never saw him shirk a task, or ever break his word.
He made a hand if riding point, or dragging up the herd.

He'd say, "Whatever trail you travel, kid,
And whatever life may bring,
Just be thankful that you're riding,
'Cause *the journey* is the thing."

23

And now I'm standing by a fresh-dug grave tears upon my face,
Listening and remembering as they sing "Amazing Grace."
My mind's eye seeing roundup camps, there with my ol' pard,
Or days spent gathering remnants in country wild and hard.
But mostly I remember his big grin at the closing of the day.
He'd wink his eye, pat my back, and then I'd hear him say,

"Whatever trail you travel, kid,
And whatever life may bring,
Just be thankful that you're riding,
'Cause *the journey* is the thing."

I've been an avid reader all of my life, and have tried to read all different types of books and authors, from westerns to mysteries to classics. My all-time favorite authors are Mark Twain, Vardis Fisher, Jack Shaffer, Leon Uris, and Dr. Suess (I can't help it; I love his books). In any book that I read I look for the "jewels" in them. One such treasure I found in Homer's "The Oddesey." The quote said, "The journey is the thing." I love that line, and it struck such a chord with me that I decided to try and use it in one of my poems. *The Journey* was the result. It seemed to touch others also; Michael Andrews, a great artist and good friend, painted a picture inspired by the poem, and my friend Leon Autrey put it to music and it made a pretty good song.

 Living life is like loading a pack mule. The trick is to keep your load "balanced."

What a Nickel's Worth

Now, we've all known men who were close with a buck,
What some folks might refer to as "frugal."
But the tightest man that I ever knew
Was a cowboy named Scotty McDougal.

We both worked awhile on the Rafter T
For ol' man Edmonds and son,
'N, Scotty was pleasant and a sure enough hand,
But he was a tight fisted son-of-a-gun.

I remember once in a bunkhouse poker game,
He was holding hearts, jack to ace.
When the dealer said, "Cards?" Scotty said, "I'll take one,"
And that ten fell right into place.

An unbeatable hand was what that Scotsman held,
But he couldn't give up his old ways.
All he could do was just call the bets.
He could not make himself say, "I'll raise."

Well, one payday, I made a trip to the outhouse.
It was an old "two-holer" out back.
And when I opened the door, there sat Scotty,
Just taking a "cob" from the sack.

As he pulled up his britches, it happened.
A nickel rolled out of his pocket,
And fell down that hole just ahead of his hand
'Though he grabbed with the speed of a rocket.

His ol' bottom lip started to tremble,
And his face got as red as a beet.
He cursed and he swore and his eyes filled with tears
As he kicked at the door with his feet.

Then what he did next was unnerving;
I figured he'd lost all control,
'Cause he reached in his pocket, took all of his money
And throwed it right down in that hole.

I said, "Scotty, what in the world are you doing?
You just throwed away all of your pay."
Swallowing hard to gain control of his voice
These words ol' Scotty did say:

"Ach, laddie, 'tis a black day.
Dame Fate is mean and she's fickle.
Yet I'll climb down in that muck, and I'll beat her again,
But, it's got to be for more than a nickel!"

In this time of "political correctness" this may not be the "in" type of poem to write, but I think that we need to find the humor in situations, and be able to laugh at each other and ourselves. The only objection that I have ever received from anyone about this poem was from a Scotsman who was in the audience at a show where I performed this poem. In the original version I used the phrase "faith and begorrah." This gentleman informed me that that was an Irish phrase. A real Scotsman would have said, "ach, kaddie." I have since repented and the corrected version is printed herein.

Tribute to Ben Johnson (1996)

You never let us down, Ben.
You always helped us see
That winning without honor
Holds no victory.

As Trooper Tyree you rode
To lead the headlong charge;
The quiet guileless hero
Whose adventures loomed so large

To a boy of youthful countenance
In the theater's dark embrace.
He rode each daring mile beside you,
Hero-worship on his face.

And as he grew to manhood
He watched you from afar,
And though you helped the hero,
To him *you* were the star.

Scandal never graced your name.
You lived the hero's part.
A world champion you will always be
In the portals of our hearts.

You always lived the Cowboy Creed,
And to mankind you were a friend.
You never let us down, pard,
And we're going to miss you, Ben.

Like most boys of my generation, I grew up watching Gene and Roy on the silver screen, and of course the "Duke." I have to say, however, that my all-time favorite screen hero was the late Ben Johnson. He seldom was the star, but was the one guy that you could count on to get the star out of a "jackpot." He made a career out of just being himself on screen. The fact that he was an honest-to-goodness cowboy didn't hurt his image with me either. I had the privilege to meet him several years ago and I've got to say that I wasn't disappointed. He was still the "real deal." I sure wish that we had more like him for the kids to look up to nowadays.

 A friend is not a feller who is taken in by "sham," a friend is one who knows your faults, and doesn't give a damn.

Bill Burk's Rx

I wrote this poem after a visit I had with my neighbor, Bill Burk.
I had my horses and mules loaded and was at the Circle K gassing
up when Bill pulled up and this conversation took place.

I saw Bill Burk the other day
And we stopped a while to visit.
He says, "I see you're still packin' them mules.
Your life's ambition is it?"

I said, "Bill, I think that it's a curse,
These cowboy boots and hats.
You try it once, you're hooked for life,
And I really think that's

"Kinda' like a vow of poverty
Them monks and friars take.
It sounds OK a-goin' in,
But the rewards are all just fake.

"I day-work every spring and fall.
I feed some when it snows.
Then wrangle dudes all summer long,
And pack hunters till that slows.

"Shoe horses for everyone in town,
Till I can't straighten up my back,
And still when tax time comes around
I've gotta go and hock my kack.

"There ain't no money in it,
That's for certain and for true,
But I just can't seem to give it up.
There ain't nothing else I want to do."

Now, ol' Bill, he mulled a bit
On this "condition" we both had.
He shook his head and then he said,
"I know the feeling, lad.

"It's a sickness lad, that's for sure;
You'll have it till you die.
It's worse than whiskey, weed, or dope,
And that's the reason I

"Think they ought to make a vaccine for it;
Just give you a shot to keep you pure.
'Cause once you get that *cowboyitus*
There dang sure ain't no cure."

 Habits are like a new hat; you have to wear them until they "feel" comfortable.

B. A. Randell

Remembering B. A.

Well, it was way up on the Double A
The first time that we met.
I was just a young vaquero,
But I still remember yet.

He was a well-respected rancher,
Earned by blood and sweat and try,
But he had the "heart of a cowboy,"
You could see it in his eye.

He asked if I could wrangle.
I says, "I've jingled in my share.
You just tell me where you want 'em,
And I'll always have 'em there."

He kinda smiled as he looked at me,
And I was scared he'd call my bluff.
Then on the spot he hired me on,
Said, "I need good hands, sure enough."

Well, I worked that summer on the A's,
And on into the fall,
My days spent learning the puncher's craft
And riding mighty tall.

I made all the mistakes that a young hand makes,
And was the butt of a joke or two,
But B. A. said I was doing OK,
And might make a buckaroo.

Seems he was always around when I'd get caught
Being the bunk house clown,
And he might laugh or grin at my dumb mistakes,
But he never put me down.

He said my cowboy skills, on a scale of ten,
Were only about four and a half,
But he said, "Kid, I'll keep you on
'Cause you always make me laugh."

Well, I left that fall, and over the years
I worked for many a brand,
And along the way I circled enough
That I finally made a hand.

I worked for B. A. two or three times
As the seasons were passing on,
And I began to notice over the years
That his best days were finally gone.

Oh, he'd still show up at the shipping pens,
Or down by the branding fire,
But his old bones just couldn't do
What was still his heart's desire.

Well, it was on the V-Slash on the desert
The last time that we met.
I was working for his boys that spring
And I still remember yet.

We were gathered at the shipping pens
It was towards the end of May.
Putting our rigs upon our ponies
At the starting of the day.

There was me and Bert and Lonnie,
And some more I can't recall,
Getting ready to make a circle
And gather them fat steers, one and all.

We'd ask young Bert about his dad,
And he says, "He's doing poorly, boys.
Just thinking about the old days
Is one of his greatest joys."

"Why, someone's here," says Lonnie
As he stepped across his kack.
We looked up to see a car pull in;
It was B. A.'s old Cadillac.

Ma Randall was behind the wheel,
And B. A. was right beside.
Just seeing the old man once again,
It filled us all with pride.

He rolled the window down a bit
And gave us each a smile.
Said, "Boys, I had to come just one more time
To jaw with you a while."

He had his old house slippers on,
And his bathrobe, too, you see,
And you could tell at just a glance
That he was sick as he could be.

He spoke to each of us in turn
As we slowly gathered round;
We was all just shuffling nervously
And staring at the ground.

Why, you couldn't catch a puncher's glance
Even if you'd try,
'Cause we was scared he'd see the mist
In each and every eye.

"You always made me laugh, kid!"
Came ringing in my ears,
But I couldn't bring myself to try that day
For blinking back the tears.

But there were tears in his eyes, too,
As he looked at all us boys,
'Cause being able to "scatter the riders"
Had been one of his life's great joys.

And when they finally pulled out through the gate
It tugged my heartstrings tight,
And I wished the years to go the other way,
And to stop time in it's flight.

But, it doesn't work that way, you see;
That ain't in God's great plan.
We've each got to play the cards we're dealt
And just do the best we can.

Well, he died that year, and it broke my heart
To know that he was gone,
But I'll bet that he's riding yet
Out there in that great beyond.

Why, I'll bet he's wagon boss on God's spread,
Where the brand's the BY N BY,
'Cause that ol' man had the heart of a puncher.
You could see it in his eye.

B. A. Randall was an old-time Arizona cowman who it was my privilege to know and to work for. He was the kind of man that was easy to admire, not only a successful cattleman and rancher, but also a "cowboy" in the truest sense of the word. In this day of "heroes with feet of sand," it is a comfort to remember men like him.

I never knew B. A. until I was in my early twenties, so the first part of this poem is from my imagination, although it captures the type of man that he was to a "T." The second part, however, is a true account of the last time that I saw him alive. It was one of those moments in time that are hard to forget.

It was my honor in 1999 to perform this poem at the Arizona Cowboy Poets Gathering in Prescott Arizona, with B. A.'s son and daughter-in-law, Bert and Garna Randall, in the audience. They cried. So did I.

 The pain of parting is the price we pay for loving. It is a price well paid.

To the Wanna-Bes

Here's to all the real cowboys,
(May God preserve the breed!)
Who cling to a life that's vanishing
And still believe in the Cowboy Creed.

Who willingly forgo the "easy way,"
And love the work more than the gain.
Who still believe in right and wrong,
And that success sometimes requires pain.

And here's to all the wanna-bes
(I'm sure God loves them, too!)
Who wish that they could do the things
They've seen the real hands do.

And though they dream of cowboy ways,
And living the cowpunchers life,
They just don't wanna-be enough
To share the toil and strife.

So, here's a toast from the real *cowboys*
To all of the wanna-bes.
Because imitation, they always say,
Is the greatest form of flattery.

The discussion about the real cowboy's vs the wanna-bes is a topic that gets discussed from time to time anywhere that cowboys gather. Real cowboys just want an honest portrayal of themselves and their lifestyle. The truth about cowboys has seldom been portrayed correctly in movies, TV, books, etc., and it rubs some folks the wrong way on occasion. My friend Waddie Mitchell said one time that "although it is an aggravation to see it portrayed incorrectly, it is also a high form of flattery that so many people want to emulate what they perceive a cowboy to be." I got to thinking about it, and I think he is right. You don't see many folks running around trying to dress like a dentist or an accountant or a welder. There is no mode of dress or identifying style for most folks no matter what they do. The cowboy is the only true icon that America has produced, and like it or not, folks want to try and have some of that mystique in their lives, too. So, y'all, "Live with it!" Like they say, "It ain't easy being a sex symbol!"

 If you appreciate 'em, let 'em know!

The Price

Have you ever watched an eagle on the wing
As he soared through an azure sky?
Watched the sun rise up behind a purple hill,
Or drop behind mountain peaks and die?

Have you watched rain clouds billow overhead,
Seen lightning dance on mesas grand,
Heard thunder snap and roll off canyon walls,
Like music played by God's own hand?

Ever lead a string of diamond-laden mules
Through an alpine meadow on a summer day?
Seen a flock of geese head south in autumn,
Or watched a deer fawn jump and play?

Have you come near death from freezing cold
Because of an early winter snow,
Or found an old reliable spring dried up
And know its five more miles to a water hole?

Ever had the bell mare take all your mules
And leave for parts unknown,
While you were deep in the arms of Morpheus
And you woke up all alone?

Did your pup chew up the britchin'*
On the new Decker** you just bought?
Ever been in a hurry to get on the trail
And one mule just won't get caught?

*Britchin'—straps that hold a saddle in place

**Decker—a type of pack saddle

Has nighttime heard you say, "To hell with this!
I'd rather be down at Murphy's Bar,"
Then change your mind in the light of dawn
As you gaze up at the morning star?

Well, I'll tell you, pard, you're not alone
With these feelings you have inside.
'Cause love and hate are just the price
You pay to be part of this tribe.

Is it worth the price, you ask me?
Has the good outweighed the bad?
Was it Heaven or Hell, or in-between,
This packer's life you've had?

Well, compadre, I'd not change a thing,
For as over the years and trails I've trod,
I've stood toe-to-toe with Mother Nature,
And I've walked hand in hand with God.

(For my pard Ross Knox who understands!
"Buenos Suerte Seimpre")

Ross Knox – Chris Isaacs
Packing Clinic, Elko, Nevada, 1998

"The Price" is a poem I wrote to try and explain the way I feel about the years I have spent making my living as a packer. No job I have ever had has given me as much satisfaction and pure love of work as being a packer. It is not easy work by any stretch of the imagination, nor is it romantic, picturesque days like you see in the magazine ads. There is a real love/hate relationship that goes with the job that is hard to explain. From quiet serenity, to sheer terror, it runs the gamut of emotions almost daily. The number one rule for a packer, I think, is, "Stuff Happens!" Believe me, it does on a regular basis. The simple trick to the whole thing is: expect it, deal with it, and don't worry about it.

My admiration knows no bounds for the packers out there. Like my pard, Ross Knox, they are truly renaissance men and craftsmen of the highest order. Besides that, they are some of the luckiest people I know!

The Saga of Cauliflower John and Truman

Now Cauliflower John is a "mule man,"
And they're a breed that's kind of rare.
They're a throwback from the old days.
You just don't find 'em everywhere.

To John, a mule is a thing of beauty;
They're a vision to behold.
(Of course John once bought an Edsel,
He was wrong there, too, I'm told.)

Sometime back John found a "dandy,"
A mule with grace and style and class.
He said his pedigree was in the "pink."
He was the "ultimate jackass."

He said, "I think I'll call him Truman,
'Cause he has that 'presidential air'."
And everyone who knew 'em said
That mule and John was quite a pair.

Things went all right for about a week,
Then one night John gets a call.
The dog catcher was upon the line
And sounded like he was gonna bawl.

He said, "Now, Mr. Phelps, I've chased your mule
For maybe a mile or more.
I've run till I'm plumb outa breath
And my feet are mighty sore.

"I chased that mule up to the fence
And went to put the halter on.
He just shook his head and jumped that fence,
And before I can blink, he's gone!

"Now, Mr. Phelps, I've got to say,
I know you think that mule has class.
But, Mr. Phelps, you need to know
He's a pain right in the ass!"

Well, John went and gathered Truman up
And took him to the house,
And for the next ten days or so
Things were quiet as a mouse.

See, ol' John went and put some hobbles on
Just to keep ol' Truman home,
But that mule loved to wander,
And that mule loved to roam.

Now the next time 'twas a neighbor
That gave ol' John a call,
And made him get his britches on
And stumble down the hall.

He fumbled with his truck keys
Then drove all over town
Just trying to find ol' Truman
And chase that damn mule down.

This time he put him in a pen
With a hot wire 'round the top.
And when ol' Truman touched it,
His eyes, they sure did pop.

This trick worked pretty well
Till this gal moved in next door.
She had a bunch of brood mares,
There was maybe three or four.

When Truman saw them mares
It was like a bolt shot from above.
Truman knew he had to jump that fence,
'Cause Truman was in love.

That dang mule jumped that fence
With just a single bound,
And "mothered up" with all them mares;
He was the happiest mule in town.

About then that lady hits the door,
And she's squalling like a cat.
'Cause she ain't a happy camper
When she sees where Truman's at.

She calls ol' Johnny on the phone
And she's as mad as she can be.
She says, "If I can find my gun,
I'll shoot that SOB."

Ol' Johnny's face got kinda red,
And his eyes turned cold and cruel.
I thought, "Ol' Johnny's had enough,
He's finally had it with that mule."

He stopped and picked his rifle up,
Then looked at me real hard,
Then turned around without a word
And headed for the yard.

I says, "Now John, don't shoot that mule,
Though I know you're awful mad.
'Cause kinda taking all in all
He's been the best mule that you've had."

John turned around with a puzzled look,
And he said, "Don't worry pal.
I love that mule with all my heart.
I'm going to shoot that gal!"

My ol' pard John Phelps is indeed a "mule man." This poem is pretty much a true story (with a small lie thrown in here and there). He owned Truman for a long time, and their relationship was the stuff of legend around our little town. Truman thought that he owned the entire town, and he simply went wherever he wanted, whenever he wanted. I don't think the fence was ever built that he couldn't breach. It finally got to be a personal challenge with John just to see if he could keep that mule in one spot for more than a week. I'm not sure that he ever did.

 To win an argument with a mule don't necessarily make you "smart;" remember that a mule is only "half jackass."

John Phelps and Jason Keith
Bottom of Little Blue River Box, 1991

The Little White Lie

I pulled in one day at the sale barn
    And saw the horseshoer's truck in the yard.
    So I pulled on over to visit,
    And make sure he wasn't working too hard.

When I got close enough to see him,
    The sight that I saw gave me chills.
    'Twas a scene out of "Dante's Inferno,"
    Made my head start to spin and to reel.

He had this ol' bay horse sidelined,
    With one hind leg pulled up and hitched.
    Over one eye was still hanging a blindfold.
    On his nose hung what was left of a twitch.

A half-empty bottle of "Ace"* lay on the ground,
    And a syringe with the needle all bent.
    Big drops of red blood on his jugular
    Showed the place where that needle had went.

His ol' bottom lip was sure drooping,
    And he had to spread-eagle to stand.
    His eyes was glazed over and sweat was runnin';
    He looked like a drummer in an acid rock band.

But, a much worse sight yet was the shoer,
    Kneeling amid tools scattered 'round.
    His shirt was in shreds and one eye was swole shut
    As he picked up some teeth off the ground.

*Ace – a slang word for Aceptomazne, a common tranquilizer used on horses.

From the end of three fingers the nails were all gone,
And the bill was ripped off of his cap.
A golf ball-sized knot just behind his left ear
Showed he'd been in a hell of a scrap.

I said, "Good night, boy, what's he done to you?
Sit down before you faint dead away."
He turned his one good eye toward me,
And these words I then heard him say.

"As a shoer, I done my duty.
I hung iron on everything that flew by.
But, pard, it wasn't because of farrier science.
It was just sweat and dirt *cowboy try*.

"See, I got a phone call this morning.
He asked, Could I do four head today?
I said, "That will just fit my pistol,
Four head at one stop, that's OK.

"He said, Now, one would need a Scotch hobble,
And one would need a blindfold.
One would take a good shot of Ace.
And one needs a twitch on his nose.

"Now, I ain't no rookie at this line of work;
I've done a bad one or two in my time.
So I told him, Don't worry about it.
Me and them horses will get along fine."

"When I got there, all four horses was tied
Right here by the side of this shed,
And I got by the first three so easy
That the fourth gave me nothing to dread.

"Now I got to admit that he didn't quite lie,
But he wasn't quite truthful either, of course.
'Cause the bad habit that each of these horses had
All belonged to the same damned horse!"

I've made a good share of my living over the years as a horse-shoer. One of the things that I discovered is that a basically honest, God-fearing man will sure enough lie to you if he has a rank horse that needs shoes and wants you to do the work. As a shoer, I've had more than one day just like the one I describe in this poem.

Thanks, Grandpa

I think back now and then on the days of my youth,
They were happy and carefree and fun.
Some of the best of them all were spent with Grandpa.
I was proud to be his grandson.

Gramps had shoed horses most all of his life;
A better shoer was dang hard to find.
Sometimes he'd take me along, though I wasn't much help,
He'd say, "I might get in a bind

"And I'll need a good handler to help bail me out
If some half-broke ol' horse just won't stand.
A good handler's important to a man hanging iron,
And my grandson here, he's a hand."

Oh, it made me feel good to hear Grandpa brag
About his horse holder when folks were around.
To hear him say that he needed my help
To me was a beautiful sound.

I'd watch every move that Grandpa would make
Around a horse with some nervous quirk.
He'd go easy, but quick, and I soon came to know
I was watching a master at work.

I'd ask questions and, Gramps, he would answer,
And though I was too young to know,
He was trying to lay a foundation
For me to build on and grow.

I asked once, "What's this horseshoe worth, Gramps?
Can't be more than a nickel or two."
He looked at the shoe, and then looked at me;
He said, "Son, that depends on you.

"If you take that old shoe and throw it back in the box
And forget that it's even around,
Why, it'll tarnish at first and then turn to rust.
After a few years it just won't be found.

"Or you can take that same shoe and nail it on cold,
Without shaping or working it any.
The chances are good that you'll cripple the horse,
And that shoe would be worth not a penny.

"But if you take forge and anvil and work that shoe right,
And trim up the foot like you should,
Well, the horse may not know it, but I promise you, son,
You'll do yourself and that pony some good.

"That's the way life worksm pard; the choice is all yours,
If you want you can just rust away.
Or like the cold shoe you can look mighty fine
And still not be worth your pay.

"But if you can take the heat and blows that life gives,
And bend, but never crack,
Then your value mounts up and you're worth a whole lot.
You can face life and never look back."

Well, I don't know if I realize yet
Just how wise my grandfather was,
But I cherish the memories I have of him now,
And I'll love him forever because

Although he was just a small-town, country horseshoer;
Never had much more than just family and friends;
But he knew about "life," and the value of work,
And how to help boys become men.

I've been asked several times if the poem "Thanks Grandpa" was about one of my grandfathers, and the answer is no. I never knew either of my grandfathers as they died before my time. The model for this particular poem was a man by the name of Clark Hunt, a good friend and neighbor for a number of years. He was also a hero to me, and I loved him like a grandpa.

 When you look into the eyes of a colt you're breaking, what you will see is a reflection of yourself!

To the Cowboy's Wife

(For Helen)

He's a "cowboy" for sure, and, pardner, what's more
He loves the life that he leads.
And though he loves her, it's true, at times she feels blue
From lack of the things that she needs.

Not diamonds or rings or other such things;
That stuff never did turn her head.
It's when he gets too involved in things that need solved,
It's the lack of attention she dreads.

And though he's handy as hell, and treats her real well,
She hates that faraway look in his eye.
He's a "tumbleweed," pard, and for him it's damn hard
Those new ranges just to pass by.

And when she wants to just sit and visit a bit
All he's worried about is the lack of spring rain.
And she just wants to balk when all his small talk
Concerns critters with high horns and no brains.

She feels she married a dope, 'cause he wants to go rope,
When a Sunday picnic would be more her style.
But she smiles and says, "Fine," as he picks up his twine
And goes to chase "corrintes"* for miles.

*Corrintes – a breed of cattle commonly used for roping stock
at rodeos, etc.

So she plays well her part and keeps hid in her heart
All these things that he can't understand.
She'll smile and she'll hide all these feelings inside
As she looks at her worn wedding band.

And she prays, "Lord above, help this man that I love,
Understand that I'm glad I'm his wife.
And help him try now and then to be just my friend;
He's already my lover, my husband, my life."

Chris and Helen, Carnero Lake, Arizona

The Scrunch

Now, family reunions are lots of fun,
There's all kinds of things you can do.
You can see all your uncles and cousins and such,
And maybe a grandpa and grandma or two.

There's always lots of good food on hand;
You can eat till you just want to pop.
Stay up all night and catch up on the news,
Just visit till you're ready to drop.

You'll see old cousins and new and always a few
That nobody's ever heard of before;
But you take the good with the bad, the happy and sad,
And throw them bedrolls all over the floor.

Now, Uncle Jim and Gramps start right in to lyin',
Don't they ever get tired of that stuff?
Cousin Ted, he teases the kids till they bawl.
Yep, he's still a "turd," sure enough.

Aunt Bertha starts in on her aches and her ills;
Says her gout is the worst the doc's seen.
She shows us a handful of colorful pills;
(I think that's what's made her so mean!)

Cousin Sally, she's brought her sixth husband this time,
And says, "this one's a keeper for sure."
Her ma shakes her head and rolls her eyes;
She's heard this baloney before!

Now, Uncle Ben, he got rich, the son of a...gun.
He won the lottery jackpot they say;
But he brags on for hours to them who will hear
About how he came up the hard way.

Then cousin Johnny comes in with a big ol' frog,
And chases the girls round the room.
Uncle Larry carries on about how tough times are,
He's a regular prophet of doom.

Now, why, I can't say, but it's always this way,
About the time you're ready to give Cousin Johnny the boot,
Why someone comes in to this chaotic din
With a camera and ten rolls to shoot.

"Now, everybody, come over here by this wall,
I need just a couple of shots."
And I never could figure how a "couple"
Meant ten or twenty as likely as not!

And then come the words that I always dread;
Makes my hair sorta stand up on end.
"Now y'all scrunch down and get in tight.
You tall ones will just have to bend."

Oh, I hate them words with all of my soul,
They make me just want to shout!
I feel like a cat surrounded by dogs
Trying to find him a quick way out.

Then suddenly one more camera appears,
Seems someone else has some photo to take.
So we sit there all "scrunched" in a wad
Like too many fish in a lake.

Now, the old folks start in to groaning,
And the babies are starting to bawl.
'Course, the teenagers already quit this wreck
Out the door at the end of the hall.

"Just one more shot," Uncle Elmo says,
And you know damn well that's a lie.
Just like Quasimodo from old Notre Dame
I've "scrunched" till I'm ready to die.

Finally the last one runs out of film
And we all breathe a sigh of relief,
But by this time I've "scrunched" for so long
That up around my neck are my "briefs."

We finally "unscrunch" and stretch out a bit
When I see Grandma start to head for the door.
"Grab her," I yell. "she's run out of film
And she's headed to town for some more!"

You know, I love my family, I really do.
They're really a fun loving bunch.
But mention reunion and I break a hard sweat
Knowing I'm gonna have to go "Scrunch!"

Family reunions seem to have some common threads running through them no matter which family we belong to. I wrote this poem after an Isaacs reunion that we held several years back. It is in honor of "Cousin Carolyn Sue," our photographia prima.

I dedicate this poem to all families everywhere, because, although we are all different, we are all basically the same. God bless the family, the backbone of civilization.

 No matter whether you look for the good or the bad in a situation, you will always find what you are looking for.

The Aftermath

This morning I walked through the door of our local co-op store
And saw a thing that filled my soul with fright.
It was my ol' pardner Kent, he was battered, bruised, and bent.
He looked like he'd been in an awful fight.

I knew that just last week he'd moved some cattle to Short Creek
So he could receive some steers on Friday night.
Now, receiving cattle can be rough when you just can't find enough
Good hands to help you keep things runnin' right.

And Thursday was Thanksgivin', and there ain't many boys a-livin'
That'll give a man much help on holidays.
Most have gone to see the folks, eat some bird and hear old jokes
And stuff their gut until their eyes just glaze.

And then the mornin' after, give out from gluttony and laughter,
They'll sneak about the house just like a Turk.
They pretend that they ain't home, and sure won't get the phone
For fear they might get caught and have to work.

So I figured he'd probably done five men's work with only one
Or maybe two more cowboys for a hand.
And that's sure a recipe for hurt or at least a maulin' in the dirt,
And a man can sure come up a-spittin' sand.

I says, "Kent, for the love of Pete, you look like you've been beat
Hard enough to put a 'crimp' in your demeanor."
He said, "Pard, you ain't got a clue of the hell I've just been through.
Why, I feel like I've just been run through the cleaner."

I says, "Did they catch ya in the alley as ya tried to take a tally
Of all them bovines comin' off the truck?
Or did you take a severe hookin' when they caught ya not a-lookin'
And decided that was when they'd run amok?"

He said, "It was awful, pard, cuz when I pulled in the yard;
They was already hot and on the fight.
They was blowin' snot and pawin' dirt and a-lookin' for to hurt
Anyone who came within their sight.

"Their eyes was ringed with red; they was fightin' their old head;
They was spooked and ready to stampede.
But I was there to try and do a job, so I slipped into this mob
To try to get it done with ease and speed.

"I worked my way in slow, trying real hard not to show
Any sign that might be took for fear.
But, pard, it was too late cuz some damn fool unlatched the gate
And they covered me up like foam upon a beer.

"They run me down just like a dog and squished me like the frog
That tried to cross I-10 at five o'clock.
I was mauled and kicked and hooked, and not one overlooked
A way to use my head for a stumblin' block!

"When the last one run on past I lay there like a broken mast
On a schooner that had been around the Horn.
And I'm here to tell ya, pard, that I ain't been used that hard
Since I seen light the day that I was born.

"And I'll just tell it to you plain, next year I'll avoid this pain
Cause I ain't goin' back no matter what the need,
The day after Thanksgivin' to K-Mart and get in on the start
Of a 'blue light special' Christmas gift stampede!"

This is a poem that I wrote after a conversation that I had with my ol' pard Kent Rollins. Kent and his bride Donna have an annual discussion about the merits of Christmas shopping (he always loses), and the need to get it done with "stealth and speed." Kent has the "common sense cowboy" approach to Christmas shopping: if you can't get it at the feed store or the sale barn, then you don't really need it! (I happen to agree with his line of thinking, but please don't tell my wife or Donna.)

Anyhow, I got tickled listening to his feeble excuses and decided that that little episode was worth a line or two.

PS Kent liked the poem. Donna didn't think it was all that funny!

Donna and Kent Rollins Chris and Helen Isaacs
Azle Texas, 1997

Memories of Grannie

Short brown hair and dancing eyes,
    A quilting frame and ginger snaps.
Crochet needles stuck in a ball of twine
    Waiting for nimble fingers to start again
And create with love, always with love.

Waking at dawn to the sound of mourning doves
    And the smell of coffee.
Evenings spent listening to the old songs:
    Billy Venero, The Haunted Hunter, Lather and Shave.
Sung with love, always with love.

Meals cooked "cowboy style"
    Meat tough and tasty,
Bread and milk in a bowl,
    Salt on the side for your onions.
Prepared with love, always with love.

That gentle voice giving encouragement.
    Gently chiding when I was wrong.
Brimming with adoration when speaking of family
    Or singing songs of praise.
Filled with love, always with love.

Knowing that I had a friend who loved me
    Then and now, as I am.
Who is waiting for me at Heaven's Gate.
    These are my memories of "Grannie"
Remembered with love, always with love.

"Memories Of Grannie" is a tribute that I wrote about my mother's mother, Evaline Lee Caffall. She was one of the strongest rocks in the foundation of my life. She was the thirteenth of fourteen children born to John W. and Lucinda Clark Lee, who were some of the first white settlers in the Nutrioso Valley of eastern Arizona's beautiful White Mountains in 1878. Her father and brothers were all cattlemen and her husband Ernest ran a small bunch of cows and packed for the Forest Service. Granddad was killed in a logging accident when Grannie was pregnant with my Uncle Calvin. She raised her children alone and often said that she had no desire to remarry. "Nobody could replace Ernie."

Grannie had a beautiful alto voice, and I swear she knew every old cowboy song there was. My mom has Grannie's old songbook with over a hundred old songs written down by her in her longhand. Mom showed it to Buck Ramsey at the Nara Visa, New Mexico, gathering a few years ago, and they were going to try and find the history and some of the forgotten melodies to some of them. Unfortunately, Buck died before they got the project off the ground.

My grannie was a strong force in my life in many ways; her independence, charity, and faith in God were attributes that I will always remember when I think of her. I can thank her also for my love of cowboy music and poetry.

The Incorrect Tally

Now, ol' Hank was "cowboy to the bone,"
Of that there's paltry doubt.
That he could ride and rope with the very best
Was a fact he'd often flout.

He understood the wild cow brute,
And outlaw horses were his "meat."
At cowboy skills and craftsmanship
Ol' Hank was hard to beat.

But, he had one glaring weakness,
And it stung Hank to his core.
This man among men with gargantuan skills,
Stood only five-feet-four.

And though he worked around this "flaw"
With his daring and his skill,
Just the thought of his "deformity,"
To Hank was a mighty bitter pill.

Sometimes he'd take to drinking
In some barroom with the crew,
And though he still stood five-feet-four,
He'd feel like six-feet-two.

Now, one night in the Bar X Bar saloon
On Springerville's "whiskey row"
When Hank and ol' Bill got wound too tight
The barkeep says, "Boys, you've got to go!"

Well, it took a bit of doing,
But them boys wound up in the street.
And they're still feeling mean and surly
As they finally gain their feet.

Ol' Hank stands six-foot-six by now,
And he's gaining inches fast.
He says, "Them boys has figured wrong
If they think of me they've seen the last.

"Ol' pard, you stand right here,
'Cause I'm going back inside.
And as I throw them varmints through the door
You count their mangy hides!"

So through the swinging doors Hank goes,
(He's six-foot-ten by now)
As ol' Bill stands ready to take tally
On the victims of this row.

Then, suddenly, like a screaming catamount
Through the doors a cowboy flies.
He lands face first in the gutter
And like a dishrag there he lies.

Bill claps his hands in pure delight,
His pard is mopping up the floor!
"That's one, Hank, keep 'em coming!"
He yells back through the door.

But suddenly he realizes
That it's Hank there in the ditch.
Hank sits up and says in some disgust,
"Don't count *me*, ya son-of-a-bitch!"

Now, friends, there's a moral to this story.
If you start to think you're six-foot-ten;
Just remember this little tale about ol' Hank,
And you might just want to think again.

Hank Sharp was a legend in eastern Arizona around the turn of the century, and stories about him are still told by the old-timers in the Round Valley area. My mother's parents, Tex and Eva Caffall, were neighbors of Hank's for many years in the small community of Nutrioso. The poem "The Incorrect Tally" was written from a story that my grannie told me years ago.

I visited with one of Hank's grandsons, Larry Rogers, some time ago, and he told me that when Hank died in his mid 90's, and they went to wash the body and get it ready for burial, that Hank still had a "hideout knife" strapped under his arm. He was truly a son of the old west.

Everybody who walks thru my door brings me happiness—some by coming, and some by going.

Cowboy Attitude

Ol' Hardtwist Ike and young Jimmy Deeks
Was making a circle one day,
Looking for "leppies" and checking some fence;
In general just earning their pay.

Ol' Ike had seen spring come for sixty-three years,
Might' near all from the back of a horse.
He was tough as a mesquite and damn near as thorny,
And plumb opinionated of course.

He allowed all these young hands weren't worth their salt.
Just didn't "bare down" near enough.
Not like the old days when if you busted brush,
You damn sure had to be tough.

He said, "You young pups are all show with your fancy gear,
Your conchos and wild rags and such.
But your chinks* is too short and your loops is too big,
They'll let ya down in a clutch!

"Ya don't tie off hard and fast? Nor use a breast collar?
How in the hell will ya handle a rank steer
Down in a manzanita thicket or a cholla patch,
Or some other spot just as severe?

*Chinks – a type of chaps

"There ain't no paw 'n' beller* in a good brush hand
When handling a wild cow brute.
You got to be tough when you're poppin' that brush.
There just ain't no substitute.

"One swing and a throw, that's all that ya get
In the middle of a mesquite thicket.
You use a short rope and tie off to your horn,
In thick brush that there's the ticket.

"You got to be tough, boy, I mean plumb 'hard'
When you ride for a 'wild country' brand.
You young buckaroos sure look the part,
But looks just don't make a hand."

Well, young Jimmy was taking this lecture in stride,
He even managed somewhat of a smile.
As ol' Ike raved and ranted about the lack of good hands,
Mile after mile after mile.

It was just about then that fate took a turn,
Disguised as a covey of quail
That flew out of a bush and under Jim's horse,
Plodding half asleep down the trail.

Well, that old bronc came apart at the seams,
And was throwing a "walleyed fit."
Poor ol' Jimmy was looking for a handle or anchor;
Hell, he'd atook anything he could get.

*Paw 'n' beller—when an ol' bull gets mad he will paw the
ground and beller to let others know he is upset.

He finally bucked out of the saddle.
So high he seen Heaven's gate latch"
Then he came back to earth, flat on his back,
In the middle of a big cactus patch.

Ol' Ike rode over and looked down at Jimmy,
He said, "Kid , are you alright at all?"
Young Jimmy smiled gamely and said, "Oh, I'm fine.
The cactus and rocks broke my fall."

Ike looked down and grinned just a bit
As he shifted the Beechnut he chewed.
He said, "Keep this up kid and you might make a hand,
'Cause you sure got cowboy attitude."

Every cowboy who has ever worked anywhere, has heard this "runnin' gun battle" about who the best cowboys are, brush poppers vs. buckaroos, dally men vs. hard and fast ropers, old time hands vs. modern day cowboys. Well the truth of the matter is that a good hand figurers out a way to get the job done whatever the circumstances, and "attitude" plays a big part.

Repentance

Now ol' Charlie was raised in a good Christian home,
They went regular to church and such.
But at the age of sixteen he fell in with cowboys,
And some others who could sin just as much.

He learned cowboy ways and became a top hand,
He knew what the cow told her calf.
But when he'd "turn the wolf loose" as he did now and then,
Why, his conscience would just cut him in half.

He'd feel low and mean and remorseful,
Then he'd have to go find him a church;
He'd go in and fess up to the parson,
And for days he'd be in the lurch.

Now one Saturday night found him in Reno,
With a redhead he just knew as "Sweet Sue."
They tried gamblin' and drinkin' and improper conduct;
They used up every sin that they knew.

Well, next morning finds him *persona non grata*,
He feels like the "prodigal son" more or less.
So he washes his face and puts on a clean shirt,
And goes to find him a church and confess.

Just on the outskirts of town he finds one,
A little white church with a steeple,
And he seen through the window as he walks up,
The inside was wall-to-wall people.

As he opened the door to slip on inside,
This deacon grabbed him by the hand.
He said, "Brother, are we ever glad to see thee,
Quick, get up there on the stand."

And before ol' Charlie could object,
He pushed him to the front of the line,
Then turned to the congregation and said,
"Our soloist got here in time."

Well, poor old Charlie started tremblin',
And his heart sorta disengages,
But figgerin' this must be part of his penance,
He just rares back and sings "Rock of Ages."

Now, old Charlie, he was a top hand,
And he sure knew bull from cow,
And his voice would make the angels weep,
But not with rapture, I'll allow.

Well, finally it was over,
And the Amen sung by the choir.
Charlie thought, "I got to give up this sinful livin',
If this is what the repentin' requires."

He thought he'd sneak on out the door;
That couldn't do no harm,
And he dang near made his getaway,
When the preacher grabbed his arm.

He said, "Son, thee should not feel bad,
Thou gave the best thee've got.
But if thee wants my true opinion,
He who ask thee should be shot."

Well, old Charlie's give up his pintoed past,
He's a model of decorum, sure enough.
It's not that he wouldn't like to sin now and again,
But that repentin's just too dang tuff.

 It's better to be prepared and not have an opportunity than to have an opportunity and not be prepared.

Remember When

It's just an old photo that hangs on my wall.
A token from a long-ago time,
Of some young buckaroos that were "curly wolf wild"
And damn sure in their prime.

Memories come so thick you can cut them
As I look at each face smiling bright.
They'd pull your rope, or go your bail,
And they'd side you in a fight.

Rough stockers all, these boys were,
And they loved the life they had.
They'd share the good times with you
And help you through bad.

In eight-second highs we plied our trade,
Then were on the road again.
Never thinking about tomorrow,
Or that those days would ever end.

But one by one we went our way
And gave up the wild and free.
My traveling pards are all housebroke now,
And all I've got are memories.

Ah, but the memories are priceless,
Of those boys from a long-ago time,
When we were all "curly wolf wild"
And damn sure in our prime.

A la vida pura, muchachos!

Left to right Norm Doyle, Bob Mareness, Joe Brown, Chris Isaacs,
Buddy Young, Buff Billings, Bobby Ski, and Bob Beaver
Mesa, Arizona, 1965

This is an old photo that hangs in my den and it is one of my prized possessions. It was taken in my folks' front yard in 1965, and it shows me and some of my old traveling pards between rodeos. They were a big part of my younger years and, although I don't see them very often, like the poem says, "the memories are priceless."

For Johnny

Where did the time go, ol' pard?
  What happened to all of the days
    When we laughed and we cried
    As we played and we tried
  To ride life to the crest come what may?

Where did our youth go, ol' pardner,
That we vowed to not let slip through our fingers?
    It seems now that you're gone
    That perhaps we were wrong,
For we both knew that time never lingers.

Where have all of the smiles gone, amigo?
Guess I've replaced them with tears.
    But when I think of you over yonder
    I have to laugh as I ponder
On the things we did over the years.

Who do I turn to now, buddy,
When the herd of life starts to stampede?
    Who'll help me get 'em to milling?
    You were the one always willing
To "bail in" whatever the need.

You were always the truest companion
And I hate it that you're not here.
    But you'd chide me, I know,
    If I tried not to show
A small grin through all of these tears.

So now it's "Vaya con Dios, compadre"
Till we ride through that "big gate" above.
   We can't send much with you
   That will help see you through,
Except memories and all of our love.

Hasta leuego, Johnny!

John Freestone was one of those friends that don't come along very often in life. My wife Helen and I shared a lot of good times with John and his wife Debbie as our kids were growing up. John was a very quiet and private man, the kind of man who didn't give his friendship easily, but when he did it was rock solid and for life.

John fought a long battle with cancer and every time we thought he was gone he would bounce back. He was a fighter. About two months before his death we went to visit him in the hospital. He looked better than he had in quite awhile, and it took me back a little when he said, "Chris, I want you to do me a favor. Write a poem for me and recite it at my funeral." Any poet knows that a request like that is a tough enough assignment, but then he added, "Make it a funny one." I said I'd try, and I did. But I found that it was hard to see the funny side of our friendship at that particular time. I apologized at his funeral for the lack of humor when I recited the poem and I know that John will forgive me; he always did. He was one of a kind and I miss him a lot.

The Saga of Lyman Beecher

(For Lyman, The World's Friendliest Feller)

In northwest Arizona, there's a place
    they call Peach Springs.
A pretty place, and over the years
    it's been known for many things.
But its claim to notoriety,
    the thing that really brings it fame,
An Indian guide, known far and wide;
    Lyman Beecher is his name.

Now Ol' Lyman is a friendly cuss;
    he visits one and all,
From day-work punchers in the spring
    to rich clients in the fall.
It seems that everywhere he goes,
    all throughout the land
Someone in the crowd will say,
    "Hey, Lyman, what's up man?"

Just drop a name,
    it don't matter who or how famous they may be;
Lyman says, "I've known him all my life,
    or least since I was three."
Well his pards got fed up
    with wild tales of Lyman's famous friends.
They says, "Next time he starts this stuff
    we'll put it to an end."

The very next day upon the tube,
    this newsman starts to tell
How evangelist Billy Graham is coming west
    to save us all from Hell.
Lyman says, "Why, Billy Graham,
    I ain't visited him in quite awhile."
Us boys all looked at each other
    and started to break a smile.

"We've caught you in your B.S., pard,
    and you'll have to pay the price.
To say you're friends with Billy Grahm,
    man, that's walking on thin ice.
He'll be in town on Thursday next,
    at the Skydome there in Flag;
I want you to introduce him to me,
    unless this is all just brag."

Well, Ol' Lyman grinned a little bit,
    even though I'd called his bluff.
He said, "You sorry sinner,
    he'll want to meet you sure enough."
Ol' Lyman's game, I'll give him that,
    with lots of guts and try.
But I had him by the short hairs;
    I knew I'd caught him in a lie.

At 7 a.m. on Thursday,
   I pulled up at Lyman's door.
Just to stop this damn name-dropping,
   I couldn't stand it anymore!
Why, he acted plumb harmonious,
   even bought a brand new hat.
He was playing this hand to the end;
   I'll have to give him that.

When we pulled into the Skydome
   them sinners was so thick
Even ol' Schwarzenegger
   couldn't a stirred 'em with a stick.
I lost ol' Lyman in the crowd
   as we was going in the door,
Thought I to me,
   "That Indian just couldn't face me anymore."

I looked all around for ol' Lyman,
   but couldn't see much from the back,
Then someone yells, "Here comes Billy."
   Now things was starting to untrack.
Now two fellers walked upon the stage
   to the applause of all the crowd,
Some was crying, some was shouting
   "Hallelujah" right out loud.

When ol' Bill begins to preaching,
   (and at that he was a whiz)
I began to cogitatin'
   just who that other feller is.
It looked like Lyman up there,
   but I knew that couldn't be,
He didn't know all them famous folks;
   this was just an O.I.T. *

So I turns to a lady standing there
   and says, "Ma'am, pardon me,
But who is that upon the stage,
   from here I just can't see."
Says she to me a-smiling,
   "I'm not sure what they call that preacher,
But that fellow standing next to him,
   that's that Indian, Lyman Beecher!"

*O.I.T. Old Indian Trick

 There always comes a time to quit talking and start acting.

The Stand-In

'Twas a sultry summer evening
    in the town of Cutters Mill,
Fireflies dancing gaily
    round the church upon the hill.

Inside the little chapel
    folks were starting to perspire
As Preacher Brown expounded
    on the wrath of God's own ire

Towards the truly unrepentant
    who flat refused God's plan.
They all were treading lightly,
    every woman, child, and man.

He said, "All men are sinful
    and deserve the Devil's lot.
Dancing for eternity
    on embers burning hot.

"There's greed and lust and envy,
    with pride thrown in to boot.
And worse than rum and gluttony
    is the love of 'filthy loot.'

"Now my brothers and my sisters,
    we're all sinners every one.
Why, I know you must be sinning
    if you're having any fun!

"Is there anyone among you
    who thinks he doesn't sin?"
He looked upon the congregation
    and gave a knowing grin.

But, then to his amazement,
    in the middle, towards the front
An old cowboy was standing.
    A bowlegged little runt.

Now, the preacher knew this puncher
    and his love for cards and drink.
He shook his head in wonder,
    not knowing what to think.

"Why, brother Bill, you think your sinless,
    free from toil and strife?"
"No, Preach, I'm just standing proxy
    for the first husband of my wife!"

Watching CNN and some of the other news networks cover the lawmakers in Washington, I've learned that these lawmakers make use of lots of things that work to their advantage. One of the little things that they use is a "proxy vote." I wasn't sure just what a proxy vote was, so I looked it up and decided that that proxy deal might sure be a handy thing at times!

Longevity Ain't No Secret

Sometimes it seems that we all try too hard
   To find what life is all about,
   Because the answer to questions like "Why is there air?"
   We could probably all do without.

But, ever now and then we run into someone
Who finds the truth very easy to see;
Who can remove all the fog from the mysteries of life
And make the puzzle as clear as can be.

Which brings us to the story of ol' Pop Jones
Who'd been a cowboy most all of his life.
He'd bid "Vaya con Dios" to all his old friends,
And had outlived all three of his wives.

So when Pop's hundredth birthday rolled around
The town figured to throw him a party,
To honor this old hand of tenfold decades
Who still met each day hale and hearty.

The town radio station, the local TV,
And big city newspaper, too.
All were on hand just to interview Pop
And find out what this old puncher knew.

"To what do you attribute your longevity, Pop?
Do you have some undisclosed mystery to share?
Has heredity given you strong genes and cells,
Or do you just handle your diet with care?"

Well, ol' Pop squinted a rummy eye
As he pondered their far-reaching questions.
He grinned as he looked at the folks gathered round,
Then made this astounding confession.

"I've lived the wild life of a cowpuncher, kid,
Where the sky was big and wide.
And I promised myself that three things I would do
Every day as I made life's long ride.

"The first thing was to eat red meat every day,
And never to have it too lean.
Then I'd smoke cigarettes, least two packs every day,
Till my breath was hard and mean.

"And the last thing I did every day of my life
Since I was big enough to choose,
Was to start every day and end every night
With at least one good shot of booze."

Well, the reporters all stared, too startled to speak,
Till one of them finally came to
And asked, "Pop, you attribute long life
To cigarettes, red meat, and booze?

"Why scientists know and doctors all say
You'll die young by ingesting that stuff."
Pop grinned and said, "Kid, all them folks that it killed
Just didn't ingest *long enough!*"

Out Fumbled

Pat and Buck were longtime pards.
  They'd run together now for years.
  They'd ranged from Pie Town* to Nogales
  And they sure knew bull from steer.

They were affable as cowboys go,
  Never missed a rodeo or dance.
  Most folks agreed they were "good ol' boys."
  You could tell that at a glance.

'Cept for their cows they shared everything
  Including the little cabin on Turkey Knoll.
  Buck's cattle were branded Rafter B
  Pat's cows ran the Double O.

Now it was well-known around our town
  That ol' Buck was a master with a rope.
  At a jackpot roping calves or steers
  Most boys had not much hope.

They'd get no laurels short of second place
  'Cause ol' Buck always came in first.
  He'd drown your quest for a championship
  Just like water quenches thirst.

So when Pat and Buck were headed home
  One afternoon in the early part of spring,
  And they came across a slick-eared calf,
  Well, ol' Buck jerked down his string.

*Pie Town—a small town in New Mexico

He says, "Pat, ol' pard, tell you what I'll do.
I'll give you a twenty-foot lead on this ride,
And who ever can get that maverick caught
Can burn their brand there on his side."

Pat looked at the calf, then looked at Buck.
He said, "Pard, I'm plumb ashamed of you.
Look down there at the end of the meadow.
That's widow Smith's milk cow, ol' Blue.

"Now I've been known to use a long rope
On a stray from time to time,
And if a feller don't get caught
I don't figure it's much of a crime.

"But, from the way that calf is marked, ol' pard,
You know that milk cow is his mama.
To steal a calf from that poor ol' widow
Would make us part of a mighty hateful drama."

Buck hung his head like a naughty child,
He said, "You're right, my pious friend.
Any man who'd steal from a poor widow
Is sure to meet with an awful sorry end.

"You've helped me see my wicked ways
And for that I thank you, Pat.
And from this day forth, pard, you can bet
A better man will live beneath my hat."

So, away they rode, this humble pair,
Buck vowing to work and pray
To cleanse his soul of iniquity...
But, soon there came the day

When these two pards were headed home;
Along that same trail they did ride,
And there in the meadow stood that same calf,
A Double O burnt on his side.

Buck's eyes got as big as a wagon wheel,
And he says, "You thievin' little elf!
After all that preachin' talk you gave
You went and filched that calf yourself!"

Pat says, "I just out fumbled you,
'Cause my mama never raised no dope.
I knew I'd better out-think a man
That I damn sure can't out-rope!"

    Pat Trainor was an old-time cowboy in the Round Valley area.
He was known to use a "long rope" from time to time, but was such
a personable fellow that he never was sent to jail for rustling
(although he was arrested for it several times). It seems folks simply
liked him too much to convict him. This poem was written from an
old story that folks tell about Pat.

The Dying Breed

I can't call myself a cowman;
    Hell, I've never owned a cow,
But I've worked for some good ones;
    some that sure know how

To make the calf crops pay the bills
    when there wasn't enough rain,
Or hold their own with bureaucrats
    and play that never-ending game.

Men whose word is binding;
    whose handshake is their bond.
They give what is expected
    and then they go beyond.

Men who understand good horses,
    and what cow mamas tell their calf;
Who take life "rough and tumble"
    and still manage a good laugh.

Whose hands are rough and rope-burned,
    who walk with stiffened gait.
Who stick by a friend through thick or thin
    and never vacillate.

Who took good care of their land
    before that was politically correct,
Who feel endowed by their Creator
    to preserve and to protect

The land they are stewards over
   and that job they took to heart.
They made their life's work ranching
   and they play well their part.

So, it's been my lot for many years
   to have worked for some of the best
Of these men who may be a "dying breed"
   yet have not shirked the test.

Who have not knuckled under
   or sold out to the corporate dragon.
Who've held the ranch together
   and still ride out with the wagon.

And I thank the Lord in heaven
   for giving me the chance
To know some of these good men
   who still work the "family ranch."

I've been in and around the cowboy lifestyle all my life. I've been a working cowboy, a day-work cowboy, a rodeo cowboy, a packer, and a horseshoer almost all of my adult life. Yet like most purists, I've been hesitant to call myself "cowboy," because I feel that title should be reserved for the folks who earn their living every day as a working cowboy. It has been my good fortune in life to have become good friends with some sure enough top-hand cowboys, and to have been included in their circle of friends. Men like B. A. Randall and his son Burt, Billy Green, and Art Lee. In my circle of poet friends, men like Leon Autrey, Curt Brummett, Jesse Smith, Sunny Hancock, Kent Rollins, J. B. Allen, Waddie Mitchell, Larry McWhorter, Ross Knox, Rolf Flake, and others who are "cowboy," have been a great influence in my life.

I take it as a high form of praise when someone calls me "cowboy," and I never argue the point. However, I am sensitive enough about that title that when I started going to cowboy poetry gatherings, I billed myself as a "Packsaddle Poet" because that's how I was earning my living. I've tried to "make a hand" whenever the opportunity presented itself, but I am always aware that a "Cowboy" has honed skills that I may not quite have mastered yet.

I'm starting to get preachy, so just let me say that my poem "The Dying Breed," was written because of the great admiration that I have for the men who make their living as cowboys. Especially those who are still trying to hold the "home place" together and fight the daily battle with not only the elements and the market, but also with the folks and agencies out there who would destroy that way of life. May God preserve them and the cowboy way of life.

The Stampede at Jenny's Cafe

I pulled in the other day at Jenny's,
A little cafe there in town.
Thought I'd get myself a tall iced tea
To help wash a burger down.

I was gettin' out of my ol' pickup
Contemplating a slice of apple pie,
When the cafe door slammed open,
And outside this feller flies.

He's wearing a helmet that looks like a mushroom,
And a pair of them spandex pants;
He's got on one of them tank top shirts,
Across the front it says "Viva la France."

Now, this ol' boy is airin' out his lungs,
And flappin' his arms about.
"Sacre bleu, vous et fou,"
I think is what I heard him shout.

His ol' eyes are big as silver dollars,
And he's blowin' rollers through his nose;
He jumps on the back of this racin' bike
And down the road he goes.

I'm wonderin', "What in the world is goin' on,"
As he peddles on out of sight.
But a hand don't have to cut much sign
To know he's on the fight.

So I goes on in the door to Jenny's
And look all around the place,
But all I see is ol' Ed a-standin' there
A look of puzzlement on his face.

I says, "Ed, what was that all about?
Seems that guy was on the hook."
Ol' Ed just shrugs his shoulders
And gives me this funny look.

He says, "Chris, I don't know what happened.
I just came in to get a bite to eat
When that feller comes through the door,
Goes to the counter and takes a seat.

"He opens up the menu
And starts gazin' at the fare;
He gets this funny look on his face
Then turns to me and stares.

"He says, Pardon monsieur, my name is Pierre LeBlanc
And I'm a stranger in your land.
Please explain to me this food called 'calf-fries.'
This term I do not understand.

"So figurin' I can educate this feller on cowboy ways
I explain about 'mountain oysters and calf fries.'
Ol' Pierre, he nods his head politely,
But I'm reading disbelief there in his eyes.

"About then Jenny comes over to take my order,
And she asks me what I need.
I says, Jenny, I think I'll just have some French fries,
And that's when ol' Pierre stampeded."

This poem was written from an old joke that my good friend Chuck Martin told me one time. Chuck and I worked together on the Aspen Meadow Ranch at the foot of Green's Peak in eastern Arizona's White Mountains for about five years. He's supplied me with lots of material for poetry, and is a great critic whenever I bounce a new idea off of him. Thanks, Chuck, for the ideas, and the great memories. Oh, and by the way, remember to "balance."

The amount of luck we have in life is in direct proportion to the amount of try we have.

Always give the best that you have got, but don't necessarily think that is what you will get in return.

Rolf's New Glasses

I was in the cafe just last week
Eating a slice of chocolate cake,
When who should walk in through the door
But my ol' pard Rolf Flake.

I said, "Hello, Rolf, how ya doing?"
He said, "Oh, I'm just doing fine.
I've just been to see the doctor,
And now I'm just killing time.

"I had to get my eyes examined,
And the Rx on my glasses changed.
I got me some of them "photo grays"
And I'll tell you, man, they're strange.

"They turn dark when you go outside.
When you come inside they turn light.
They even come trifocaled.
Heck, you can wear 'em day and night.

"Oh, guess I'd better go,
I just seen my wife walk by.
Why, I just can't wait to drive,
And give these things a try!"

I said, "OK, I'll see you Rolf,"
As he goes to catch up with Jean.
Then the feller in the next booth says,
"Them new specks your pard got are keen!

"Them glasses are really something.
I think I'll get me some of those.
But, do you think they'd sell me a pair
Without the mustache and the nose?"

One of the great things about cowboy poetry events are the friends that I have made. Rolf Flake is one of the poets that I met at a gathering years ago. He has become a dear friend, and he sure puts up with a lot from me when we perform together. We have a great time taking "shots" at each other on stage, and the poem, "Rolf's New Glasses" was one I wrote a while back. We have had a lot of fun with it. He is a great guy to travel with, if you don't have to share a motel room with him (he has been known to snore a little, but that's fodder for another poem). Thanks for your friendship, Rolf...see you at the gate!

 Good friends are one of God's greatest blessings.

The Cowboy

(For Colton)

I had ol' Fooler at the saddle house,
And was puttin' my outfit on.
The air was still and smelled of sage
Like it usually does at dawn.

Three heifers in the Bennett trap
Had dominoed* yesterday,
So I figured I'd ride over there
And head 'em in this way.

I heard footsteps behind me
So I turned around to see
This pitiful looking cowboy
Just staring back at me.

His chaps were worn and ragged,
His rope had broken strands.
I guess he'd missed some dallies
'Cause he had Band-Aids on his hands.

His boots was on the wrong feet,
And one spur was all he had.
He dang sure weren't no beauty;
His looks was awful bad.

His ol' hat was way too big,
Which made his ears protrude.
His fly was unzipped, but I said nothing
For fear he'd think me rude.

*Dominoed—slang for giving birth. To domino is to replicate.

His shirttail fluttered in the breeze,
Untucked there in the back,
And as he raised his arms to yawn
You could see his ol' butt crack.

His nose was skint and scabbed up,
Like he'd been in a fight,
And I have to say in honesty
He was an awful sight.

Now, if the cowboy dress code means a thing,
He was about the worst I ever saw.
But I knew that he was sure a hand
When he said, "Ets doe dit dem tows, Papa!"*

*Let's go get them cows, Papa.

At this writing, I am the proud "Papa" of eleven grandkids, and
as any grandparent will tell you, "my grandkids are the greatest."
They all like to ride the horses and play cowboy when they come to
see us, but I've got one three-year-old grandson who is "eat plumb
up with cowboyitus."

I worked for a while on the Bar Flying V ranch in eastern
Arizona, which is the setting for "The Cowboy." This poem is
almost exactly the way it happened that morning, and as we rode
along, with him in front of me in the saddle, I got that lump in my
throat that can't be explained, only felt by someone who has
received the ultimate validation of his lifestyle. Thanks, Colton!

Freedom Lost

(For Monk Maxwell and Them Like Him)

I've seen sad and forlorn faces
Of every type and size.
From looks of pure frustration,
To red rimmed, tear stained eyes.

A heart-broke child I once observed
Who'd just lost a balloon.
I've seen an egomaniac
Made to look like a buffoon.

A broken-hearted lover
I once saw shed big tears.
And the ones he couldn't wipe away,
Was falling in his beer.

I've seen a wheeler-dealer "blanch,"
When he couldn't close a deal,
And a worried look in my cousin's eyes
As they read my uncle's will.

But the most pitiful look I ever saw,
Or ever hope to see,
Was on the face of a five-year-old, renegade steer
That was necked to a mesquite tree.

 When you're through learning, you're through!

Michael Bia

You spent your childhood wild and free,
And none of us could then foresee
How you'd touch our lives, or to what degree.
We never knew you, Michael Bia.

Your life was in the land and sky;
Vermilion cliffs and mesas high.
These were yours to occupy.
You were of Diné,* Michael Bia.

The White House called; you left your land,
And off you went to Viet Nam,
To a war you did not understand.
You did your duty, Michael Bia.

You fought with honor and with pride,
But before the fighting could subside
In that far off land, you died.
You gave the ultimate, Michael Bia.

At Window Rock in sixty-eight
They turned a bull out of the gate,
And his bell rang loud to reiterate
Our thank you, Michael Bia.

Diné, and white men, too
Stood and shed a tear for you;
And though your time on earth is through
May God keep you, Michael Bia.

*Diné is what the Navajos call themselves; it means "The People."

Now often when I think of the past,
Or cross that reservation vast,
Or see Old Glory at half-mast,
I think of Michael Bia.

Ya'at'eeh, Hastiin! (Ya-ta-hey, Has-teen!)

There are things that happen in our lives that we have absolutely no control over, which become a part of us forever. Such was the case with the poem about Michael Bia.

I got out of the U.S. Marine Corps in January of 1967 just as things were really starting to heat up in Viet Nam. Michael Bia was leading the bull riding standings for the AIRCA when he was drafted and sent to Viet Nam just about the time I was discharged. He never came home.

In 1968 my wife Helen and I were at the Fourth of July rodeo in Window Rock, Arizona, where I was entered when something happened that haunted me for years. The Navajo tribe paid tribute to Michael Bia at that rodeo by taking his chaps and spurs and attaching them to a bull with Michael's bull rope and then turning the bull loose in the arena during a moment of silence. Nothing has ever affected me quite like that short moment of tribute to a fellow cowboy/comrade-in-arms, and I have thought of it many, many times over the years. One sleepless night several years ago as I sat in my den, the first stanza of the poem popped into my head from out of the blue. As I sat there the words just kept coming and I wrote the entire poem in a matter of a few minutes which, I assure you, is not the way that I usually write poetry. I felt that something special had happened, and it was so personal to me that I didn't share the poem with anyone for a long time. The first time that I tried to recite it, I broke down and cried, which kept me from trying it again for quite a while. Then in 1997 at the Elko Cowboy Poetry Gathering I was on the Veterans Session with Joel Nelson, Rod McQuery and some others, and managed to get through the entire thing. I have reached the point where I can recite the poem without showing too much emotion, and it has become one that I recite fairly often.

It has been interesting to me the things that have happened because of the poem. I have had many Vets thank me for the poem, which means a great deal to me. And although I never knew Michael Bia, I have met some of his family, and I feel a real bond with them, and through them, with Michael. I did a show near Washington, D.C. a few years ago, and made it to the Wall (the Viet Nam Memorial) where I found Michael's name. Then in 1999 some friends of mine presented me with a rubbing of Michael's name from the Wall. In a strange way Michael has become a friend.

At the end of the poem I use the Navajo phrase "Ya'at'eeh, Hastiin! (Ya-ta-hey, Hasteen!)" which is a greeting. I have been asked a couple of times why I used that instead of the word "hágoónee´" which is the word for good-by. My only answer is that I never met Michael, so it just didn't feel right to say good-by. And when I do meet him I hope to greet him with a "Ya'at'eeh," the same as I would any old friend.

 Give without remembering; receive without forgetting.

Life's Split

I'm sure you've heard at least once in your life
Of some horse that couldn't be rode.
The *Bad Brahma Bull* or ol' *Zebra Dun*,
Or some cowboy who couldn't be throw'd.

The *Cowboy in the Continental Suit*
Who made the boys all gawk,
Or other twisters, bad broncs, and outlaws
Who fueled that cow camp talk.

Well, this story ain't one of them kind.
It's not about being the best.
It's just a story about a bull and a kid
Both trying to pass life's test.

They crossed paths a half dozen times
Over about four years or so,
And it made the kid smile to see #30
By his name at the start of the show.

Now, ol' #30 was a crossbred bull
That would turn back either way.
He was honest and true, a bull rider's bull.
The kind a hand would want any day.

The first time they met was in '65
At the big show in Casa Grande.
Ol' #30 was there just doing his job;
The kid trying to make a hand.

Both bared down as hard as they could,
And when the eight seconds was through
The kid had won the buckle that day,
And thought he was a top "buckaroo."

The next meeting took place in Kingman
And #30 evened the score.
The kid thought he'd just had an off day,
And he was dang sure ready for more.

The bull won next, then the kid took a turn;
Now the score was two to two,
'Cause to ride was to win on ol' 30,
But if you'd falter, he'd bid you "adieu,"

The next time they faced each other
Was on California's Golden Shore.
And though the kid hung tough for five or so,
It was ol' 30's turn just once more.

So, they drew around each other for almost a year,
Then the Orange County fair came around.
Sure enough, when the kid checked the draw,
By his name #30 was found.

And as he sat on the bull pen's top rail
His mind's eye thought of the past.
He thought of the eight-second battles they'd fought,
And wondered, "Today how was the die cast?"

Chris Isaacs on #30 Laguna Beach, California
May 21, 1967

Well, ol' 30 bucked good, and the kid made a hand
And was still there when the buzzer did sound.
He picked up his check and went on down the road
Wondering where they would meet next go-round.

But the next go-round never did happen.
'Twas a drama that never would play.
The next time the kid checked on the draw
The secretary said "Ol' 30 died yesterday."

Well, the kid misted up just a little
As he thought back over the years.
On rides won and lost on the back of this foe,
And he wasn't ashamed of his tears.

Like I said at the first of this story
It's not about being the best.
'Cause the bull and the kid both gave their all,
And fate just took care of the rest.

"No winners?" you say. "They need a tie-breaker.
Someone has to come out on top.
It's un-American to just break even
Then bring the whole thing to a stop!

"Society says...You have to be number one.
Anything else means you're just second-rate.
To lose is a blight upon your name.
You should live to vindicate..."

Well, friends, here's the truth from my point of view:
"Give your best and expect the same back in the end.
'Cause a fifty-fifty split ain't a bad average, pard.
And a worthy opponent is almost as good as a friend."

So many poems have been written about bull rides that I swore years ago that I would never write one about bull riding. So much for saying "never."

Lloyd Hawkins had a bull back in the '60s that he called #30. He was a big gray crossbred Brahma bull, and he was sure a good draw. You could win on him if you got him rode, but if you stubbed a toe, he would dang sure buck you off. I drew him six times over about a four-year period; I won on him three times and he bucked me off three times. He was sure one of my favorites and I felt bad when he died.

I've thought a lot about him over the years, and while this may not be a particularly good poem, the sentiment comes from the heart. (And I promise, I won't write any more bull riding poems!)

 Difficulty may be the price of a real blessing.

The Heart of the Rodeo Clown

This poem is dedicated to Buck Croft, Tommy Lucia, and especially to Buddy Young, who were good bull fighters and better friends. Thanks, guys!

Most folks know the role of the rodeo clown
Is to save the poor bull rider's hide,
But there's another side to the man in the wig
That can help if you're making the ride.

He can take that ol' bull and turn him around
Or just let him buck out straight,
And a good clown will ask the man on the bull
What he wants when they open the gate.

He'll grab for a horn or maybe an ear
And turn him back left or right;
He'll help that cowboy by talking to him,
Yeah, he'll help with all of his might.

And if the twister can cover the bull
And get to the pay window, fine.
The clown will just grin at the cowboy
And say, "Sure, pard, any ol' time."

Oh, he'll take his lumps when saving a hand
Whenever a bull's got them down.
But helping the other fellow look good,
That's the "heart" of the Rodeo Clown

And as we perform in the Arena of Life
I think God would approve if we could
Take that lesson from the rodeo clown,
And help the other fellow look good.

Answered Prayer

They say the Lord loves little children
  and I believe that's true.
I think he understands them
  and the prayers of kids get through.
That simple childlike faith is real
  and the Lord,he understands,
And He really does hold children
  in the hollow of his hand.

I remember when my two oldest,
  (we call 'em Sis and Bud)
Were playing out back by the ditch
  in the water and the mud.
Well, Sis came in crying,
  upset with her little brother;
And so, like kids are want to do,
  she went to tell her mother.

"Bud locked me in the playhouse, Mom,
  and he wouldn't let me out.
I yelled for you or Daddy,
  but you weren't nowhere about."
"Then how'd you get out, sweetheart?"
  her mother asked so gently,
Wiping tears from freckled cheeks,
  and listening so intently.

"Oh, Heavenly Father helped me out,"
came the simple quick response.
"I prayed and asked Him for some help,
    just like you told me once."
Intrigued, her mom asked,
    "Well, hon, what happened then?
Did God come by and unlock the door,
    and set you free again?"

With a puzzled look Sis replied,
    "No, He wasn't anywhere about.
But He reminded me there was a window,
    so I went and kicked it out."
Happenstance, or a small miracle?
    I just don't have a clue,
To that little girl 'twas answered prayer,
    that's for certain and for true.

And I think maybe there's a lesson there
    for those of us who've grown
Too wise and smart to listen
    when God answers from His throne.
We should be like little children,
    he way the Lord wants us to be.
To listen just like kids, when He said,
    "Let them come unto me."

The Lord wants to help us
    even when we think He's nowhere about,
If we just bow our heads and ask his help,
    then kick that window out.
Dear Heavenly Father, hear my prayer,
    it comes right from the heart,
Help me have the faith to ask, Lord,
    and then be ready to do my part.

Bud and Sis, Mesa, Arizona, 1973

I never cease to be amazed at the life lessons that we learn from kids. They have a way of cutting through the bark on the tree of life, and getting right to the heart. The poem "Answered Prayer" was inspired by a little incident that happened when my two oldest kids, JoAnn (Sis), and Robert (Bud), were having a little spat out back of the house. As near as I can remember Sis must have been about four or five years old and Bud about three. The lesson she taught Helen and me that day was a profound one. The Lord wants to help us, and will, *but*, I think that He also expects us to bail in and do what we can, and then He'll take care of the rest.

God bless the children, and may God grant us the humility to continue to learn from them.

 The two best gifts you can give a child are "roots and wings."

Ol' Pancho

Why did you kids drag that thing home,
  He'll just be a nuisance, I bet;
Tear up trash all over the yard,
And run up a bill at the vet.
Another worthless, damn dog.

Yeah, he's fuzzy and cute, but he'll grow up, you know,
And won't be like he is today.
So don't get attached, I don't want you to bawl
When he goes and runs away.
Sorry, whining, damn dog.

Say, that's a pretty good trick that you taught him, son,
But I bet he won't look at a cow.
He'd just scatter the herd and get in the way,
But I guess you can keep him for now.
Good-for-nothing, damn dog.

You know that mutt didn't do too bad today,
Helped keep the herd bunched up tight.
And did you see the way that he worked that ol' cow
When she got on the fight.
He might be OK, that damn dog.

He's sure good in camp, come the end of the day,
Never begs or acts like a pest.
Stays by me all night at the foot of my bed,
Keeping the watch while I rest.
I kinda like that damn dog.

Now, you don't let critters into your heart;
They're just a commodity.
You can't get emotionally tied to a dog,
But with him I come close, you see.
He's all right, that damn dog.

I came home yesterday from a trip out of town,
And they told me Ol' Pancho had died.
I had to go to the barn on some pretended chore,
So they couldn't see when I cried.
Lord, I'll miss that damn dog.

Lisa Issacs and Pancho
Rudd Knoll near Big Lake, Arizona

I've always thought that "Ol' Shep" type of poems were sappy, and didn't figure that I'd ever write one. That was before Pancho came along. He truly was *my dog.* He couldn't stand to be far from me, and would pout like a kid when I would leave him home. When I would start to load the truck and trailer for a pack trip he would drive me nuts until we finally left.

I had to make a trip to Utah in January several years ago and didn't have enough room for him in the cab and it was just too cold to let him ride in back. I put him out of the truck three times that morning, and the last time I got after him awful hard. When I got back a week later he was dead from poison. You can imagine the mind games I played over that. The "what ifs" drove me crazy for a long time.

He was a great camp dog; always stayed outside the kitchen area, and would never make a pest of himself in camp. He had a unique way of letting me know when something was around at night. He never barked, but would get by the head of my bed and growl very low until I woke up. I've never had one quite like him before or since. He was a dandy.

 A good hand is always in the right place at the right time.

Thanks (I Think)

"Well, it's still snowing I see,"
He growls as he gets out of bed.
He slips on his boots and his wild rag
And pulls his Scotch cap down on his head.

He curses softly as he wades through snow
And enters the barn hallway;
"Looks like this damn frozen fluff
Just might be falling all day."

He mumbles and gripes as he wipes away snow
Then pulls down a three-wire bale.
His frozen mustache now has more ice
Than the end of ol' Roanie's tail.

He swears as he grabs the axe handle
And heads for the frozen horse trough.
He figures he'll die of pneumonia
As he hacks out a lung-wrenching cough.

The holes in his gloves let the ice in
To help freeze his fingers some more.
"Damn this cold and this damp," he exclaims
As he stomps off the snow at the door.

He mutters as he pours him some coffee
And throws some bacon into the pan.
He thinks of some place like Tahiti
Where in the winter time he'd need a fan.

Then he moves his plate to the table
And bows his head to say grace.
Then finishing says, "Thanks for the snow, Lord.
We sure need the moisture here on this place."

I live in the White Mountains of eastern Arizona. It isn't the type of place that most people think of when they think of Arizona. The elevation is seven thousand to eleven thousand feet and the pine and aspen trees are here in abundance. However, it is an area where the average rainfall is only about seven to eight inches a year, and if we don't get sufficient snowfall in the winter we are in serious trouble. There is an old saying around these parts, "You can cuss the mud, but not the rain or snow." But along about February and March I sure get tired of the snow, cold, and wind. I guess I was feeling that way when I wrote this poem.

THE WIND BLOWS SO HARD HERE THAT THE
SNOW DON'T GET A CHANCE TO MELT...
IT JUST WEARS OUT!

 As you travel the trails of life always remember that no matter where you go, there you are!

The Trade

The fall rains had been good that year;
  The winter temperature plumb mild.
  It's the kind of year a desert cowman loves
  'Cause the feed comes fast and wild.

We'd been in camp about two weeks,
  Puttin' out salt and fixin' fence.
  And when them Mexican steers arrived
  The cowboyin' did commence.

We was brandin', tippin' horns, and vaccinatin',
  And pardner, I ain't jokin'.
  We worked them steers so smooth and fast
  We had that squeeze chute smokin'.

Then we scattered steers in every pasture,
  Till, pard, when we was through
  That piece of Arizona terra firma
  Looked just like a bovine zoo.

We was about two days from bein' through
  And changin' horses at the holdin' pen,
  When through the gate in a cloud of dust
  Comes our neighbor's boy, young Ben.

This boy's daddy had a rep as a trader;
  He could trade the wings right off a moth.
  And the word around was that young Ben
  Was cut from the same durn bolt of cloth.

His stock trailer was plumb loaded down
With some chickens, a goat, and two sows.
A litter of mangy-lookin' pups,
And one brown Swiss milk cow.

The kid said his "howdys" to all us boys
Then zeroed in on the boss.
He says, "Mr. Bill, I'm in the mood to trade,
'Cause I need a saddle for my hoss."

Well, the boss looked in the trailer,
Shook his head and says, "I don't see how.
There ain't nothin' in that trailer that I want,
'Cept maybe that ol' milk cow.

"That is if she gives a lot of milk,
'Cause fresh supplies are gettin' mighty few.
We might trade a saddle for ol' Bossy,
If you'll throw in a layin' hen or two.

"But, now, that cow's gotta' be fresh,
And easy to milk, you understand.
And she's gotta give a lot of cream
To satisfy this sissy-lookin' band."

The kid shook his head and said, "Mr. Bill,
You drive a hard bargain, and that's no trick.
And sure as I'm born I'm windin' up
With the short end of this stick.

"But, I'll trade your way this time,
And it'll be OK, I've got a hunch.
But just to sweeten up the deal,
How 'bout if you throw in lunch?"

The boss grinned plumb down his sleeve
As he drug out that ol' worn-out wood.
It was dry and cracked and weather worn;
He'd hung that kid out but good.

Well, the kid unloaded Bossy gently,
And throwed his "new" saddle in the back.
He turned and said, "I hate to admit this,
But I just had a guilty conscience attack.

"'Cause truth to tell that ol' cow's a bandit,
And I guess you'd better know it now.
Though she's full-growed, she's never been weaned,
And I caught her suckin' one of my cows."

Well, the boss just looked up and grinned
And said, "Kid, the laugh's on you.
We ain't got nothing on this place but steers.
That ol' gal's milk stealin' days are through."

We all had a good laugh at that,
And then went to fix some eats.
Warmed up some coffee, beans, and bread,
And other cow camp treats.

Suddenly ol' Bob says, "I'll be damned,"
While holding stifled mirth.
'Cause that ol' cow had her head under her flank
Sucking herself for all she's worth.

The kid looked up from his plate of beans
And says, "Yep, she's a robber, that ol' cow,
And even though this is a steer operation,
She's suckin' one of *your* cows now."

The late Ben K. Green was, in my opinion, one of the greatest cowboy storytellers that ever lived. In one of his books titled *Wild Cow Tales*, he had a story about a cow trade that was too good for me to pass up; I had to try to put it to rhyme. So, with apologies to Ben, I wrote "The Trade." Anyone who has ever watched two "traders" try to outdo one another will appreciate the story if not the rhyme.

Justice or Mercy

It seems the life of the cowman is forever intertwined with his banker, and there are few in the banking business nowadays who really understand the cattle industry or its needs. This poem is just a tongue-in-cheek "shot" at the bankers from a cowboy's point of view.

A banker woke up dead one day
And found himself at the Gates of Pearl,
So he knocked in anticipation
For the eternities to unfurl.

Saint Pete himself answered the knock
And asked the banker what he wanted.
"Why, I've come for my Eternal Reward,"
Said the banker quite undaunted.

Said Pete to the banker, "Not so fast,
Although you think you're setting pretty;
Your case is not quite cut and dried.
You'll have to go see the Committee."

So down an alabaster hallway
The erstwhile banker ambled.
Thought he, "They'll surely let me in,
I hardly ever womanized or gambled.

"I only charged what the law allowed.
The Federal Reserve made all the rules.
Prime rate plus fifteen was my motto.
It's not my fault those folks were fools.

"My books were always to the penny;
As bankers go I was a prince.
That embezzlement charge wasn't proved.
There was no concrete evidence."

Then, at a hand-carved door he paused.
"Entrance Committee" a gold plaque read.
An angelic receptionist ushered him in
To a sight that filled his soul with dread.

There at a table sat three folks
With whom he'd dealt before.
He tried to beat a hasty retreat,
But Saint Pete had closed the door.

The first one was the widow Brown
Whose house he'd repossessed.
Next in line was ol' Ned Fisher
Who'd given him money to invest.

The last one on the committee
Was the rancher, ol' Buck Macon.
"Why, I loaned him dough for years.
Perhaps he'll save my bacon."

So the banker sweated bullets
While The Committee read his file.
They cast sideways glances at him,
But gave neither frown nor smile.

Then the widow Brown spoke up.
"Your terms were always tough.
For such a stingy soul as yours
Hell's fire is not enough."

Ned Fisher chimed in with a shout
"Hell's imps could learn from you
How to deceive and cheat and steal
And then smile when you were through.

"There's nothing that they have in hell
That could repay your malevolent deeds.
You bled mankind to the last drop
With your self-serving needs."

But then, up spoke ol' Buck Macon
And said, "Friends, don't hold a grudge,
Just because he made us toe the mark
And on terms he would not budge.

"Justice or mercy should be our goal,
And on that we must agree.
In his time on earth he showed no mercy,
So by the rules, then neither can we.

"But we can and must give justice,
So to my plan please lend your ear.
Let's sell him my ranch back on earth,
And then give him *ten dry years*."

If Dr. Seuss Had Been a Cowboy...

(With apologies to Dr. Seuss)

In the deep shady canyons far below Concho Peak
Billy the Bull was the King of the creek.
A swell little creek with plenty of shade,
Just the kind of a place where a bull had it made.
There was plenty of grass and the water was cool,
If a bull left this place he'd be branded a fool.
Everything was right here that a bovine might need
And ol' Billy knew that he was lucky indeed.

Till one day Billy peeked out of the brush on the creek
And saw a small knob known as Paradise Peak.
"This creek where I live is way too low down.
I should live higher up," Billy said with a frown.
"If I lived on that peak, how much greater I'd be.
Why, I'd be the king of all I could see.
Other bulls would be jealous of the place where I'd play.
I'd only come to this creek just to drink, once a day!"

So Billy the Bull threw a "nine"* in his tail;
He bellered and pawed and ran up the trail
Till he came to the top of Paradise Peak.
He cried, "Why, up here I can see for a week!
This canyon and peak I'll rule all of my days.
Other bulls will be awed by my wondrous ways.
I'll blow snot and beller and tear up the turf.
I'll proclaim this my kingdom for all that I'm worth!"

*Nine—When a cow or bull gets excited and starts to run, the
animal has a tendency to throw its tail up in the air and over its
back; the curl in the tail resembles the number nine. The
expression to "throw a nine in his tail" simply means that he is
excited and running.

"I'll breed three heifers a day, right here on this peak.
Oh, glorious me, that's twenty-one every week!
I'll be the He-Bull on this whole big wide range,
Bossin' cows and steers and bulls that are strange.
I'll tear up the bushes, knock down all the trees.
All the bulls on this mountain will wish they were me."
So, all of that day he pawed the top of that hill,
And chances are good he'd be pawing there still...

But, he made so much racket and raised such a din
That three canyons over, an ol' cowboy named Jim,
(Who lived in a cabin made of peeled logs, of course)
Had heard him that morning while saddling his horse.
Now, wild maverick bovines were what Jim liked best;
To chase, rope and brand 'em and all of the rest,
Cause Jim was a waddie who knew how to catch strays.
Heck, he'd been doing this job for most of his days.

So, Jim checked his cinches and took four hoggin' strings,
A runnin' iron, prunin' saw, and several more things
That might come in handy when he got the bull caught.
He'd take care of the whole deal right there on the spot.
He eased his ol' pony up out of the creek,
Stuck his head round a bush, just to get him a peek
At Billy pawin' dirt and throwing dust in the air;
Jim says to himself, "This don't hardly seem fair."

But, he wasn't the kind to pass up a gift horse,
So he stepped off and tightened his cinches, of course.
Then mounting his pony with a cowboy war whoop,
He built to ol' Billy and cast a big loop
Which piled round the horns of this vocal bovine;
Then he laid him a trip and tightened his line.
Well, that laid poor ol' Billy right flat on his back,
The victim of a sure enough "cowboy attack."

The hoggin' string went on like a song at a dance,
So quick that ol' Billy had nary a chance
To even think of escaping or getting away,
And Jim's hot iron and knife plumb ruined his day.
When the artwork and surgery were finished at last
Ol' Billy's demeanor was completely downcast.
Three heifers a day was now only a dream;
No longer the captain, he's just one of the team.

So, listen my friend, if you're the Bull of the Woods
Don't beller too loudly if you've got the goods.
Don't swagger and blow and raise too much hell,
'Cause the truth of the matter is you never can tell
When some waddie like Jim will ride up your trail,
Jerk down his twine and put a kink in your tail.
Just live quiet down there in the cool and the shade,
'Cause the truth is, pard, you may just have it made!

IF DR. SEUSS HAD BEEN A COWBOY!

Every now and then I find an author whom I admire so much that I want to try and write something using his particular style. It is always done for fun and with apologies to the author. The late, great Dr. Seuss of children's books fame is certainly one of my heroes when it comes to poetry. He was a master of his craft, and had an unsurpassed imagination. His stories and poems were simply *FUN*. I have often thought that he would have had a great time writing cowboy poetry, so when he passed away, I decided to write a cowboy poem using his story line from "Yertle the Turtle" as a pattern, and trying to copy his style. I have to say here that it was much harder than I thought it would be. To be silly and frivolous, and make a valid point all at the same time is no easy chore; as I found out, but, trying to "write like him" is almost as much fun as reading what he wrote. Now that I think of it, writing and reading poetry should be *FUN*! That was what Dr. Seuss was all about. I hope he would be pleased.

*Chris Isaacs and Baby Doll just above HU Bar
headquarters on the Blue River.*

The Blue

This country's big and rough and wild,
 It's not for the faint of heart.
 But for those who want a place unvanquished,
 Mother Nature's done her part.

 The Mexicans who ruled here for centuries
 Simply called this place "Azul,"
 And, pard, it's one of the brightest diamonds
 Encrusted on God's footstool.

 They say Coronado passed this way
 In his quest for gold.
 Geronimo and his band rode these hills,
 Or so the story's told.

 Ben Lilly ran his pack of hounds
 Beneath these canyon walls;
 He knew its secret places,
 Each seep, each waterfall.

 Clell Lee rode these draws and ridges.
 His horses rattled their hocks
 From KP* down to Squaw Creek,
 Stray Horse to Jackson's Box.

 Freddie Fritz built his home on the river;
 He called it the "Triple X."
 My Grandpa Caffall ran a pack string here.
 Most folks just called him "Tex."

*KP – name of a ranch

135

These and a few more hardy souls
Who have fled the haunts of men,
Have sought its rugged beauty
To find solitude again.

Now, it's my turn to ride these trails,
To gaze in wonderment and awe
At the grandeur and the beauty
In each canyon, ridge, and draw.

Like these men who came before me,
(And I know this must be true)
I thank God Almighty
For this place they call "The Blue."

It has been my privilege in this life to have been a packer in
some of the most beautiful country in the world, most of it right
here in Arizona. Arizona is not the place most folks think of when
they think of pack trips, but we have some of the finest back
country you can find. Of all that I have been in, my favorite is "The
Blue." My mother's people were some of the first white settlers in
this part of Arizona Territory, settling in Nutrioso, just west of The
Blue in 1878. Her dad was a packer for the government, and
worked the Blue for several years. It is still a wild and rugged piece
of country, and I'm thankful that I have been blessed to be a part
of it.

Chris Isaacs

Our talents are a gift "from" God. What we do with those talents is our gift "to" God.

Wisdom Comes With Age

When I was a young handful of brashness and pride
I used to swagger and boast of the ones I could ride.
Make 'em sixteen hands tall, I don't care if they're rank.
I'll "air" them dudes out if they turn the crank.

The old hands would grin at my "ranahan" ways
And hoped I'd get smarter one of these days.
Well, now I'm an old hand, and I'm smarter of course,
'Cause what I really crave now is a *short, gentle horse.*

As I have mentioned in a couple of my other poems, I am
having a hard time adjusting to my "advancing years." It makes me
angry that I don't seem to be able to do what I once could. But
every now and then something will happen that puts it in
perspective. In the summer of 1997 I had a bronc flip over
backwards with me and send me to the hospital. He was one of
those type of horses that my friend Larry McWhorter would call
"unrepentant." I was about three months healing up, and spent a
good deal of that time planning my "revenge." When the day
finally came, I caught him and saddled him up and went back in
the saddle house to get my chaps and spurs. I was standing in the
doorway looking at him when it occurred to me that what I was
contemplating was not only stupid and self-serving, it was
dangerous. Hell, I was fifty-five-years old and he damn near killed
me last time; and besides, after three months he sure wouldn't
know what was going on. I stood there for a long time trying to sort

out my thoughts; kind of a "reason vs. ego" contest. I finally decided that I didn't really have anything to prove; I had ridden my share of broncs over the years, and this was nothing more or less than ego and revenge. I turned him out, but in my gut I felt I had played the coward.

It was a long time before I worked up enough courage to even tell anyone about this little episode, and it was my friend McWhorter to whom I finally confessed. Larry is sometimes wise beyond his years and is one who understands both horses and men, and what he said to me that day made me feel a lot better. His observation was, "That wasn't cowardice, Chris, that was wisdom." I sure hope that he was right.

 Check your back trail every now and then to make sure the pack string is still there.

You can't change the past, but you sure can learn from it.

Change is usually hard but it ain't necessarily bad.

God's Canvas

Just north of the Escudilla
I paused a while tonight
And watched the Master Painter
Turn the daylight into night.

I stepped down off my pony
And just stood there on the rim,
Watching as the canvas changed
At the Almighty Artist's whim.

The colors were so brilliant;
Fiery reds to deepest blue
Would change to pink and purple
Right there within my view.

It was more than just a vision,
For mere man almost too much.
The hand or eye was insufficient,
'Twas for the soul to touch.

My horse and dogs felt it, too.
They seemed to understand
That a masterpiece was being built
By the brush in God's own hand.

For the rain that fell this afternoon
Had left a fragrance that was there,
Of wet dirt, sage, and cedar tree.
It hung heavy in the air.

You see, the colors on God's pallet
Touch more senses than just sight,
And His mighty brushstrokes fill us
With both insignificance and might.

Then, as I gazed there in amazement
At the beauty that I saw,
My soul filled to overflowing
With the wonder and the awe.

God gave one final brushstroke
With his Almighty hand,
And day was gone as darkness fell
Across this blessed land.

Arizona is known worldwide for its beautiful sunsets, and those of us who have lived here for years sometimes take them for granted. While coming home one evening just north of the Escudilla Mountain, I saw a sunset that just took my breath away. As I sat there the words to this poem started to come so fast that I had to write them down then and there. I have only had this happen to me a couple of times in my life, and it was a unique experience for me.

I have always been amazed at God's handiwork, and this particular experience was so powerful that it was almost a sacred sensation. I truly thank my Father in Heaven for the privilege of having made most of my living out in his magnificent masterpieces.

VT Cabin on The Blue

Line Shack Memories

The dry hinges whine out a protest
  as I open the old bunkhouse door.
My boots make a sad hollow cadence
  as I cross the worn wooden floor.

My eyes adjust to the dim light
  and I slowly look all 'round the room
That once held gay, laughing cowboys,
  but now has the feel of a tomb.

The ol' stove's now a home for pack rats
  and the bedsteads sure look a fright,
But I remember how good they both felt
  on many a cold winters' night.

I pull up a chair at the table,
  just to rest for a moment or two;
My mind starts to drift back to old days
  when I'd lived here as part of the crew.

Ol' Sunny and Jesse both worked here a while,
  then spooled their beds and moved on.
Ross rode the rough string here one winter,
  but come spring he was married and gone.

Why, I can almost hear Leon telling ol' Kent
  as they played two-handed "pitch" every night,
"Damn it, Kent, you can't trump that!"
  and you'd think they was fixin' to fight.

And ol' Tommy cooked many a good meal
    when us boys came draggin' in about dark.
Hot biscuits and beef, coffee and pie;
    his cookin' sure did hit the mark.

Well, look up there above the doorjamb
    it's the brand Donnie burned on the wall
The winter we hired on to gather the steers
    the boys had missed in the fall.

Let's see, that was the winter of '68;
    oh, no, surely that can't be so.
Why, I remember it like it was yesterday.
    Has it really been that long ago?

Then the memories start to weigh on me
    like the plunder I'd load on that ol' pack mule.
Tears well in my eyes and start to roll down the cheeks
    of this damned sentimental old fool.

So, I close the door with reverence
    as my ol' heart starts to swell in my chest,
And I thank the good Lord for the privilege
    of havin' ridden with some of the best.

Anyone who has ever lived "in camp" for any length of time will most likely relate to this poem. I had occasion to go by myself back to a camp where I'd spent a lot of time with others a few years ago. It is a fourteen-mile trip on horseback to get to this particular camp, and not many people even know where the old cabin is. I'm thankful that there are still a few places like that around, and that I got to spend some time in them.

It was an odd experience in that this was a place that was always full of life, and now was silent and full of memories. I seem to wax more and more nostalgic as I grow older, but sometimes the memories are almost as good as the real thing.

 The silence of an empty house can sure be "loud."

The Offering

The trail climbs up through the oaks,
  Then turns out by a red rock wall;
  I stop my horse to let him blow
      And look down through the cedar trees.
  A black plume rises from below,
  Turns to gray, then fades and drifts.
  Until at last it becomes nothing,
      Like a specter on the breeze.

What I did was not done in anger
  Or in hatred of anyone.
  It was done in love and honor
      Of ways that are dying each day.
  I step down off my pony
  And walk to the canyon rim;
  I gaze out at draws and ridges
      As my memory starts drifting away...

To a time when a fuzz-faced kid
  Looked down from this lonely vista
  And gazed in awe at God's handiwork,
      Absorbed in Arizona's glory.
  The old man there with me grinned,
  Said, "It's something ain't it, kid?
  You know, if this country could talk
      She could tell us quite a story.

"My dad settled here in seventy-six
When Apaches still ruled the land,
But he treated them fair and honest
       And their ire he never dreaded.
He carved out the old headquarters
Back where we started this morning,
Next built Spring Camp on Blue Ridge;
       Then Cottonwood Camp where we're headed.

"He died over there by them Chalk Cliffs.
That was April of nineteen and ten.
We was gathering slicks at Bull Durham.
       He just slumped in his saddle and died.
I took over then and here we are
Still trying to make this place pay.
So jerk on them mules and let's move,
       We can make camp before dark if we try."

That was the first of many lessons
I learned from that old man.
Lessons of history, cattle, and honor.
       Of hard work, blood, sweat, and tears.
Then, like the young do, I drifted
To new ranges, bright lights and life.
But we kept in touch, and our friendship
       Has lasted through all these long years.

So, I wasn't surprised by his phone call
Early one morning last spring.
He said "Kid, I just needed to visit
      With someone who will understand.
I've given my life to this place, Kid.
I never wanted anything else.
Now people who have never been here
      Want to take over the land.

"They've cut my permit to nothing,
And then raised the grazing fees.
Spotted Owls now owns the high ground,
      And the gray wolf will soon reappear.
Riparian areas seem to abound,
But not for my cattle to drink.
And cattle are not welcome to graze
      On feed wanted for elk and for deer.

"I've fought 'em kid; God, how I've fought.
But I'm losing, that's plain to see.
Oh, I'm old and my ways are sure dying;
      Maybe I'm just tired of the fight.
But, today in the mail comes a letter
Advising me of a new study.
They've decided they need Cottonwood Camp
      For a new administrative site.

"Well, I guess I've bothered you enough.
I just needed someone to hear.
Come visit an old man sometime, kid.
      You know your welcome on this brand."
Two days later I got a message:
The old man had died in his sleep,
Peace on his face and a photo
      Of Cottonwood Camp in his hand.

So, here I sit watching the smoke
Rise up from the valley below,
Leaving only ashes at Cottonwood Camp,
      A haven for cowboys and cattle.
Well, they can't have it for an "admin" site.
There's no way that I could allow it.
And I know they'll probably win the war
      But me and the Old Man won this battle.

    I was hesitant to include this poem in a book, as it will probably offend some folks. I didn't write it to offend anyone. I wrote it to try and explain the feelings of some people towards what is happening in the west today. I hope that the sentiments can at least be understood if not condoned.

It's Enough

With a well-practiced eye, I surveyed the kid
Who had ridden the hurricane deck.
He had scored 86 to the roar of the crowd
To win both the buckle and check.

The announcer said, "Now there's championship style.
That ride just made him five grand.
This cowboy life ain't a bad way to go.
There's big money in being a hand."

And my mind drifted back to those long-ago days
And the pards that I'd traveled with then.
I thought of the boys that I'd rodeo'd with.
Hell, we're now just a bunch of old men.

Why, when I first cracked out "ol' Case" was on top
Just spurrin' them broncs with high style.
With his lavender chaps and his practical jokes;
But ol' Casey's been dead now a while.

And remember ol' red-headed Billy Kornell,
Won the world in, I think, it was sixty-two?
Let's see, that'd make him over fifty-years-old!
Oh, hell, boys, that just can't be true.

Say, remember Vegas back in sixty-five
When ol' Bob was the first rider out?
He scored 88 spurrin' the hair off a "wasp,"*
Gave the rest something to worry about.

*Wasp—a horse that bucks quick and snappy.

But I seen Bob a while back, and he's old and fat
And his hair is sure getting thin.
Then I looked in the mirror and I thought to myself,
"How'd we get in the shape we're all in?"

And I hurt every morning when I roll out of bed
With them ol' broken bones just aching.
Then I thought of all the ol' pards just like me
And the bruises and lumps we'd all taken.

I think back on good broncs and bulls that we'd rode
And I laugh, even though it ain't funny.
We must have done it because we loved what we did;
It sure as hell wasn't the money.

And I think I'm plumb jealous of these modern day hands
With their big money and sponsors and such.
We rode just as hard and traveled as far;
Surely we deserved just as much.

But then, I reach under my belly and touch that ol' buckle,
And reflect on them times, smooth or rough.
I've got memories and friends and some old eight-by-tens,
And I'll tell you true, pard, it's enough.

I wrote this poem after a trip to Las Vegas to watch the National Finals Rodeo. Many things have sure changed since the 50s and 60s. I admire the hands today; they take it a lot more serious than we did, I think. They are more businesslike about it. But, you know, although the hands today make a lot more money, I don't think for a minute that they have as much fun as we did !

This is also the first poem that I ever recited in public, "for hire." It was at the New Mexico Festival of Cowboy Poets, and one of my heroes was in the small audience, Buck Ramsey. He came over to me after my set and shook my hand and said, "I sure like that poem." I left the hall feeling ten feet tall and bulletproof!

 Old age ain't for sissies!

You can choose to be happy, or you can choose to be miserable, but the "choice" is always yours.

The Last of the Breed

(For Uncle Claude)

A crisp fall breeze blows gently,
Causing gramma grass to wave
Around the feet of silent mourners
Who stand near an open grave.

Sweat-stained hats held in hands,
Black wild rags at their throats;
Scarce hearing words meant for comfort
By a preacher as he quotes

Things meant to help, and though they mean no insult
By hearing not his words;
Their thoughts are on their pardner,
The last who'd trailed to Magdalena with the herd.

A page of history had turned today,
No more within their view.
The stories can no more be told
By one who really knew.

Tales of wild horses and wilder men,
Rank steers and outlaw cows
That made the drive to Magdalena.
They are only legend now.

Those who bore their comrade to his rest
Know they bury here today
A part of yesterday that's gone forever,
So they bow their heads and pray.

"Lord, we're sending home a puncher,
And if You might could try
To find a place out with the wagon
On that range up there on high,

"And if by chance You're shipping, Lord,
Why, have your cow boss pass the word,
And you'll have one more good hand to drive
To Heaven's Magdalena with the herd."

"The Last of the Breed" is a poem I wrote about the old Rail Head Driveway that was used by the cattlemen in eastern Arizona and western New Mexico from the late 1800s until about the late 1940s.

My uncle, Claude Lee, was one of the last of the old-timers who had made the drive to Magdalena on a regular basis. I wrote this poem as a tribute to him and to what used to be when he died in October of 1994 at the age of ninety-six.

Old Ned and Claude Lee
1898–1994

To do what we like is freedom. To like what we do is happiness.

Big E's Jiffy Boot Repair

(For my pard Ellis)

Several years back I was punchin' for hire
On a spread out Springerville way.
I spent a cold winter snappin' out broncs,
And earning a good puncher's pay.

When spring finally came I was ragged and worn,
I looked like the frayed end of a rope.
I had patches on holes, and holes in them patches.
Seemed a new wardrobe was my only hope.

I goes into the drygoods and buys several shirts,
Four pair of Levis and a new Stetson, too;
And I figured I'd buy me a new pair of boots,
'Cause my old ones had the soles wore plumb through.

But, aside from the soles, them boots weren't too bad,
So I took them to Big E's Jiffy Boot Repair.
I says, "E, while I'm breaking in these new 'kicks,'
Slap some soles on this old worn-out pair."

About two days later I got a call from a pard
Who was working out West Texas way.
Said they needed a good hand with talents like mine,
And if I'd come, hell, they'd double my pay.

Why, I loaded my plunder in my old Ford truck,
And headed east before you could say "boo."
I forgot all about them old boots of mine
As down Highway 60 I flew.

Well, two years went by 'fore I headed back west
To Arizona and that Springerville town.
I was looking for old friends and maybe some work,
If there happened to be any around.

Now, as chance would have it, as I pulled into town,
The first thing I seen was this sign.
It said, "Big E's Jiffy Boot Repair. One Block West,"
And I remembered them old boots of mine.

I thought, Now I doubt if them boots are still there,
But, still it might be worth a shot.
So, I pulls up and stops and goes in the front door,
To see if maybe them boots E's still got.

Well, Big E's in the back as I mosey on in.
He looks up and says, "Yah, whatcha need?"
I says, "E, I'm embarrassed to ask you about this,
But to my foolishness I must concede.

"About two years back, I left some boots here,
'Cause my socks was rubbin' the ground.
But, until just this minute, I'd forgot all about 'em
Do you suppose they might still be around?"

Big E thought, and then said, "I'll go look in the back,"
And I knew that the outlook was bleak.
But Big E came back in and said "Yep, they're still here,
And I should have 'em ready for you sometime next week."

Choose the Right

Good Morning Lord, I'd like to visit
If you think you've got the time,
And talk about a thing that happened
That's sorta weighed upon my mind.

I won't bother you with tales of sinful living
'Though I probably really should.
I just wanted to let you know about a thing
That I feel done me some good.

You know I quit the Bar D outfit
And thought I'd move on to other range.
I was traveling through this little town
When something happened that was strange.

I seen all these cars and trucks
Parked around this little country church,
And it dawned on me that it was Sunday.
Guess my mind was sorta in the lurch.

I hadn't been to church in many moons
'Though I ain't got no good reason why,
But I got a feeling that I ought to stop
And give this little church a try.

As I parked my pickup at the curb
I could hear the sweet refrain
Of a hymn I'd never heard before
And I didn't know its name.

But its words, they cut right through me,
Its message clear and bright;
"When a choice is placed before you,
Always choose the right."

"Choose the right," what a simple thing,
Yet the message is profound
'Cause even in the life of a cowhand
Many answers must be found.

Which cows to keep and which to ship
Don't seem like no big thing.
But it sure does make a difference
In your calf crop come next spring.

Or trying to start a good young colt
And you're wantin' to do it without a fight;
I reckon that slow and steady and consistent
Is one of them ways to "choose the right,"

And I guess the real test must come
In how we treat our fellow man,
'Cause "choosing the right" in our dealings
I'm pretty sure would be your plan.

And I reckon that forgiveness
Would be in your plan, too.
'Though sometimes our durnb pride, Lord,
Makes that awful hard to do.

Well, I don't remember too much else
That was said in church that day,
But I thank you, Sir, for listening
To what I've had to say.

And thanks for leading me by that little church
Where that sweet hymn cut through the night.
And, Lord, please help this sinful puncher
Always try to "choose the right."

(*Choose The Right* is the title of a favorite old hymn.)

 Be careful if everything is going your way.
You may be headed in the wrong direction!

Viejo

I turned Viejo out the other day,
  Our season's work is through.
He'll be on good pasture now till spring
And then we'll start anew.

That ol' mule has been a dandy,
'Though he's getting long in the tooth.
I've never asked what he wouldn't give,
And that's dang sure the truth.

For thirty-one years he's earned his keep.
He always gave his best.
For making a circle or packing a load,
He always passed the test.

With a nervous dude or a little kid
I never had to worry.
Ol' Viejo never took a wrong step
Or ever got in a hurry.

Any packer that ever threw diamonds
Has wished for one like him.
Whatever plunder you wanted to take
Would get there safe and trim.

And I wondered as I took his halter off
When I turned him loose at the gate,
Would he winter OK just once more,
Or was his time running late.

And I thought, "Ol' man, you're the best.
You're the 'diamond' in my string.
And if God will grant it one more time
I'll see you in the spring.

"But if He needs another pack mule
To reach those heavenly mountain crests,
And he calls for you, I'll understand,
'Cause I'm sure God would want the best."

I bought a crippled mule several years ago that was on his way to the killers. I knew the history on this mule and thought that as a horseshoer I might be able to save him. It was a long shot, but it turned out to be some of the best money that I ever spent ($200). I called him "Viejo" which is Spanish for "Old Man," and he was a favorite of my two youngest kids, and anyone else that I ever put on him. He was a pack mule extraodinaire; never tightened a lead rope or made a bad move. I used him for three more years after I wrote this poem, until he was about thirty-five-years-old, then turned him out for good. He lasted about two more years running with the mares. He was a dandy, and I wish I had a pastureful just like him.

Michelle Isaacs and friends on Viejo, 1995

It's damn hard to beat a "journeyman" at his job!

The right "hitch" for the type of load your hauling is the trick for getting it to camp.

The Cowboy and the Indian

By chance they came together,
    One to teach and one to learn;
    The student to gain knowledge,
    The teacher to impart.

In time they came to know each other
As Human Beings,
Along the trail
And around the campfire

Both bespoke their pride
In the legacy of their forefathers.
The teacher's blood of nations mixed,
The student's proud and pure.

The teacher asked prying questions,
The student answered from the heart.
Both parted better people
From the knowledge that they shared.

Now the cowboy has new insight
Into the Indian's real world.
The Indian has a new skill
To add to his life.

Both have learned.
Both are more knowledgeable.
Both have received a precious gift.
Both have a new friend.

It is "Washta." ("Good" in the Lakota language.)

Clair St. Arnaud and Chris Isaacs
VT cabin 1996

Clair St. Arnaud was a student in one of my packing schools. He is a full-blooded Lakota Sioux and very proud of his heritage. He is a world-class iron man tri-athlete, and has two college degrees. Not the kind of person you would expect to find in a class where you teach folks to "lash and load." In the ten days that we spent together we developed a strong bond; he became a real friend. I truly believe that he taught me more than I taught him. Thanks, Clair.

The Crew

The first rays of dawn are just lining the ridge
  As the fuzz in my head starts to clear,
The chime of the bell mare's hardware declares
  That the mules and the horses are near.

I wave away all the cobwebs in my head
  As I catch my first glimpse of the sky,
And the red glow that spreads over clouds in the east
  Speaks of rain before this day has gone by.

Ol' Chili Beans letting me know with a bray
  While I pull on my boots and my pants,
That he's ready for his morral* full of grain
  As he stomps out an impatient dance.

Snowball and Ike both know this routine;
  Content to just stand there and watch.
Ol' Truman stands back far away from the rest
  Determined that he won't get caught.

Viejo snorts as he sees me stand up
  As if to say, "I'm all ready, pard."
And Ol' Pancho, my pup, goes and pees on a tree,
  To let 'em know he's the top dog in this yard.

I get my chores all finished and done
  And build up the fire good and hot,
Warm up the coffee that's left from last night.
  Too lazy to make a fresh pot.

*Morral – feed bag

Guess I ought to slip hobbles and halter 'em up;
Get sawbucks untangled and set.
Hang all of my plunder and get it lashed down;
But, damn it, I ain't ready yet.

J. J., my saddle horse, just raises his head
Then swings his tail at a fly.
He senses my mood; he's seen me like this
In plenty of days gone by.

Guess I'll just let 'em rest a short while more.
Heck, we ain't in no big sweat.
And I'll tell you the truth about this bunch:
They're the best that I've had yet.

It takes a while to make a good string;
To get 'em so they see
How I work, what the pecking order is,
And what they can expect from me.

I'll just kick back for a short while yet,
'Cause I'm right proud of this mob.
You can't beat a journeyman at his trade,
And these boys can sure do a job.

So I'll watch my coworkers eat their grain
And scratch my ol' pup's faithful head.
Drink my second cup of last night's bitter brew
And remember what that Bible verse said.

Genesis 1:25

"And God made the beasts of the earth after their kind and cattle after their kind, and everything that is upon the earth after their kind; and God saw that it was good."

As a packer, it has sometimes been difficult for me to explain to people how I feel about my animals, and especially my mules. Mules have had such a bad rap for so many years, and in my opinion it is mostly unearned. "The Crew" is my attempt to say how I feel about a good string. The animals named in this poem were some of the best I've ever had.

The Flying Horse

As a cowboy "making a circle"
You can see some funny things,
But the strangest one I ever saw
Was a horse that sprouted wings.

It was way up on the Hulsey Bench
When the summer grass was high;
One of those days so filled with beauty
It'd bring a tear right to your eye.

I was riding ol' Spud and leading a mule,
Packing in a load of salt,
When a bend in the trail brought to my eye
A sight that made us halt.

There in the meadow asleep like a babe
Laid a big ol' buckskin mare.
She was dreaming the dreams of the pure in heart;
She didn't have a care.

She must have filled her belly in the cool of the morn
And when the sun got high
She found her a sunny spot to sleep
And just dream of the by-and-by.

Now the thing that was odd about this scene,
That would get your attention twice,
Was off to the side stood a big black crow
Just as cool as summer ice.

The ol' crow seemed perplexed, he wasn't quite sure
If the mare was alive or dead.
So he hopped to and fro all around ol' Buck
From her tail plumb up to her head.

Now where to begin on this pleasant repast,
The ol' crow sat there and thought.
To start at one end and just work my way through,
That's the best way as likely as not.

Now if I start at the head I'll run into them bones,
And they're mighty hard on my beak.
But if I stick to the soft parts and bypass the rest
I ought to have him gone in a week.

So Mr. Crow hopped around to the back of ol' Buck,
Just to find him a good place to start.
He looked up and down from the hip and the hock
Just to find him the tenderest part.

Now, with ol' Buck stretched out like a stiff on a slab,
It sorta left her tail stickin' out in the air.
And right there underneath seemed a good place to begin;
Why, there wasn't even no hair.

Mr. Crow looked again and said to himself,
"Oh, my, is that a bullseye I see?
I swear, that shows me right where to start,
And the best part of all, it's plumb free!"

So, without further ado, he raired back and pecked
And hit that bullseye right there on the dot,
But his joy turned to horror when Buck's tail clamped down
And Mr. Crow realized he was caught.

Ol' Buck quit the earth like a space shuttle flight
Just leaving the launching pad.
To be woke from her dreams in just such a fashion.
I figure it drove her plumb mad.

She jumped, she bucked, she whirled, she kicked;
She was clearing the tops of the trees,
With that ol' crow's head clamped tight under her tail
And his wings just fanning the breeze.

Now the higher she'd buck, the harder he'd flap,
And they both had something they wanted to lose,
But the harder he'd pull, the tighter she'd clamp;
It was kinda like one of them "catch twenty-twos."

'Course from where I was sitting it was easy to see
How ol' Buck could've cured all her ills.
If she'd just lifted her tail and broke wind real hard
She'da blowed that crow plumb over the hill.

But when I seen 'em last they was tearing down trees
And clearing the brush, far and wide;
Ol' Buck trying to pinch the head off that crow,
And him just a whippin' her hide.

Like I said at the first, as a cowboy at work
You can see some peculiar things.
But the strangest thing I ever saw
Was that horse that sprouted wings.

"The Flying Horse" is a poem that I wrote from a story that my dad told me years ago. Dad came to eastern Arizona with the CCCs in the 1930s and wound up in the Nutrioso Valley at the foot of the beautiful Escudilla Mountain. The Hulsey Bench rises just outside of Nutrioso, and was the easiest way to get to the summer pasture on Escudilla. Dad day-worked and cowboyed for the local ranchers, and spent a lot of time on the mountain. He has some great stories from that time in his life, but this one was always one of my favorites.

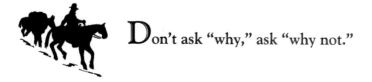 Don't ask "why," ask "why not."

Angels Camp

(In Memory of Buck Ramsey)

There's a starlit trail
Where the moon never pales
That winds up to the Great Divide.
It's a trail that's seen
In a cowboy's dreams
Where only the Good Hands ride.

Through passes, past fountains
Of God's sacred mountains
It winds to a valley serene.
To a camp that is there
In a meadow fair
Where the grass is lush and green.

There's a chuckwagon there,
And a small coulee where
The remuda grazes nearby.
A group of Heaven's top hands
Who ride for this brand,
Are gossiping under the fly.

And around the campfire,
If you were to inquire
Of one of this heavenly cowboy throng,
Why so many were here,
He'd just grin ear to ear
And say, "We rode in to hear Buck sing a song!"

Vaya con Dios, Buck.

Caption J. B. Allen, Buck Ramsey, Chris Isaacs
Nara Vista, New Mexico, 1886

"Angels' Camp" is a poem that I wrote in memory of a great poet and good friend, Buck Ramsey, who died in January of 1998. Buck was one of the first people who gave me encouragement where my poetry was concerned. He was always ready to give advice or a kind word if it was needed.

Buck had been in a wheelchair for years when I first met him, and when he died I could not get the picture out of my head of Buck "standing up" to perform. The more I thought about it the more I knew that if he had a choice, he would be singing not at a great concert hall in heaven, but to a bunch of friends around a campfire in some heavenly cowcamp.

Buck was one of the most unpretentious, down-to-earth people I've ever met. Like the Bible says, "He was a man without guile."

Vaya con Dios, siempre, Buck!

 A good friend never asks "why" you need help; he asks "how" can I help?

I Think I'll Be a Cowboy Poet

I think I'll be a cowboy poet,
   And say the things they say.
   I'll get invited to them "gatherings,"
   'Sted of out here pitching hay.

I'll grow me a mustache like ol' Waddie,
   That'll curl up on the ends.
   One that'll set me apart from the "common" crowd,
   And make me the envy of my friends.

I'll want a delivery just like Baxter's
   With a voice that's low and rough.
   I want to tell about "Oysters" and "The Buckskin Mare,"
   And other such brain-teasing stuff.

I'll tell my poem straight from the heart.
   I won't just "paw and beller."
   I'll turn a phrase just like McCrae,
   That cowboy story-teller.

My meter and rhyme I'll want to be tight,
   Crisp and clean, like Mike Logan's,
   When he writes about the "Shaman's Hands,"
   Or such other fancy slogans.

Just take these few talents and "wad 'em" together
   And add a few more just for fun.
   It won't take long till I'll be the "He-Bull."
   Why, I'll be "Number One."

But...

My facial hair don't grow too well.
And I got a voice like a squeaky gate.
I'm plumb scared to tell a story in front of a crowd.
And my meter's always running late.

So, I guess that wasn't a very good plan.
You just can't be something you ain't.
But, say, them cowboy artists do pretty well.
I think I'll go buy me some paint!

It has always been a source of wonder to me how people can change their likes and dislikes in fashion, music, hobbies, and so on whenever a "new craze" comes along. I guess I'm not much for big change in my life. I remember when I went to my twenty-year class reunion; I ran into a girl that I had gone all through grade school and high school with. She came over to me and gave me a hug and then, holding me at arm's length, she said, "Why, Chris, you haven't changed a bit." Then looking at me a little closer she said, "I don't think you've even changed clothes!" So much for being a slave to changing fashion.

Anyhow, the point I'm trying to make is that after the first Cowboy Poetry Gathering at Elko and it's huge success, all of a sudden anyone with a big hat who could rhyme "how" and "cow" was a cowboy poet. Now before you grab a rope and start looking for me, let me say that anyone is welcome to write anything that they want. The poem "I Think I'll Be A Cowboy Poet" is just my tongue-in-cheek jab at those folks who change their lifestyle every time the wind swaps direction. It was meant to be a humorous look at human nature. Really!

Mutual Respect

Down on "The Blue" where the canyons run deep
And the mesas are both steep and high,
The cattle run wild and they stick to the brush.
It's a place that most punchers won't try.

But, ol' John Bennett and his pardner, Bob
Were at home in this devil's playground.
They rode rock-pounding horses, and had cow-savvy dogs;
Better "brush hands" were dang seldom found.

They decided one winter to work Rousensock Creek,
And camp at the old VT* shack and corral.
So, they load all their plunder on a half dozen pack mules
And start into this cowpunchers' hell.

Now most good plans have one or two flaws,
And the glitch in this one was a mule named Lightning.
She was smart as a whip and mean as a snake;
A combination most hands would call frightening.

With her feet, ol' Lightning was quick as a cat;
She could kick the wings off of a fly!
She'd bite, she'd buck, she'd refuse to get caught.
She'd aggravate you and not even try.

But, the worst trick she had, the one that brought tears,
Was when she'd fall back on the lead line.
'Cause then she'd bust loose and scatter the string;
She'd caused many a wreck in her time.

*VT—VT Ranch

But ol' John was a thinker, and prone to use tricks.
He wasn't about to let that mule rule the trail.
He bought a shock collar, like dog trainers use,
And attached it to ol' Lightning's tail!

He said, "Now, Bob, you take the control, and I'll take the lead,
And when you see that ol' mule start to do it,
You just give me a holler and I'll dally up close
Then you take this buzzer and pour the juice to it!"

So, off down the trail this mob perambulates,
One dummy, six asses, and a fool;
John just waiting and Bob anticipating
The education of their "electrified" mule.

Well, it wasn't too long till school was in session
'Cause ol' Lightning was planning to bolt.
But a surprise like she was fixing to get
She ain't had since she was a colt.

She picked her spot and put on the brakes,
But ol' Bob was paying attention.
He yelled, "Here she comes, John," and then hit the switch.
Which sort of started a stuntman's convention.

When that spark hit her tail, ol' Lightning broke wind
And jumped right in the saddle with John.
Then the whole damn "wad" went over a cliff
And before you could blink, they was gone!

Well, John, his horse, and ol' Lightning
All went flying off into space.
Left Bob up there on top of that bluff
With an incredulous look on his face.

In disbelief he watched them do a "halfgainer"
And land in a big cedar tree,
Ol' John just a-screaming, "I ain't ready yet, Bob."
And discussing that mule's pedigree.

Now, as cowboy wrecks go, on a scale, "good" to "bad"
This one only rated "just fair,"
'Cause John was only six weeks in the hospital,
And only five days in intensive care.

Well, now John and ol' Bob are back working The Blue,
And ol' Lightning, she still works the trail,
But she stays right in line and she don't balk at all.
And John, he don't put one damn thing on her tail!

A good friend of mine by the name of John Bennett cowboyed
for several years in the Blue River country of eastern Arizona. They
used lots of mules in that country, and being a mule lover myself
and having worked the same area as a packer, I grinned from ear to
ear when John told me this story. Cowboy logic has been the
subject of much conversation over the years, but I think that this
story tells the tale about as well as it can be told!

She'd bite, she'd buck, she'd refuse to get caught.

Fuzzy Memories

(For Buddy & Beve)

Recipe for retrospection:
Take two old rodeo cowboys
Add several stories about "the good ol' days"
Pour in one case of beer
Mix well and enjoy "Fuzzy Memories."

Old Buddy and Beve were reminiscing
About the lost days of their youth,
When they were wild and rough and ready,
And just a little bit uncouth.

Recalling broncs they rode and girls they'd squeezed,
And fights that had went for days.
They spoke reverently of Prescott, and Boulder,
Where they'd both had winning ways.

Bud said, "Remember '65 in Brawley?
Now that one was a little bit rough,
'Cause it wasn't just in the arena
Where we done that cowboy stuff.

"Why, them hotels and barrooms,
They was quite a sight to see,
'N' what the tourists liked about it
Was that show was all for free.

"Why, with the drinkin' and the fightin',
And them other manly sports,
You'd see hands and dudes and buckerettes
Of every size and sort.

"Say, remember that durned elephant
That showed up at the dance?
With ol' Larry on him bareback
As round the floor they pranced!

"How 'bout when we throwed Walt out the door
Wearin' nothing but his hat,
With a quart of ol' Jack Daniel's whiskey
In the hallway there he sat.

"Man, I can still hear him holler,
'Damnit boys, this ain't as funny as you think.
When I get back in I'm gonna kick your...
Oh, howdy, Ma'am. Care for a little drink?'

"But, Beve, the best trick done that week,
Or at least that I recall,
Was when you bet the boys that you could fly.
I swear, that sure beat all.

"You bet 'em all a hundred bucks
That from your second story nest,
You could fly plumb around the hotel
And not once stop to rest.

"Why, that bunch of drunken cowboys
Covered your hundred in a flash,
Then the side-bets started flyin'
Like a cook aslingin' hash.

"You took one more shot of whiskey
And was out that window with a bound;
But, pard, you dropped just like a cow turd
And sorta splattered on the ground."

Beve said, "Yeah, I do kinda remember that.
It wasn't the smartest thing I ever done.
Things have a way of gettin' out of hand
When your havin' too much fun.

"And, anyhow, you was standin' by the window,
Why'd you let me dive on through it?"
Bud said, "Hell, I had ten bucks on you myself,
I thought that you could do it!"

My two old travelin' pards, Buddy Young and Bob Beaver are
the characters in this poem which I took from an old story that I
had heard years ago. While the second story "flight" didn't actually
happen, of course, most of the other things referred to in the story
are true. I don't see Beve and Buddy often anymore, but I love
them like they were my brothers. I've got a world of friends, but
none better than these two.

Buddy Young, Bob Beaver, Chris Issacs

Fred

My heroes have always been cowboys,
Just like ol' Willy Nelson said.
And so it's always been with me,
You see, my hero's name was Fred.

As kids in school we ran together,
You'd not see one without the other.
Our friendship knew no bounds.
We thought that we were brothers.

He was always there when I needed him;
Somehow he always knew.
We depended on each other.
We were amigos through and through.

He taught me about good horses
And how to be light with my hands.
Showed me how to work a pen of cows,
To read the earmarks and the brands.

He'd say, "Work slow and ease on in
When you ride into the herd.
If you start to chouse and fight 'em
They'll get ringy, take my word.

"If you take your time and do it right,
Why, once will be enough.
Just take each job as it turns,
Then move on to other stuff."

He could always calm me down
When I'd get on the fight.
He helped me see the wisdom
Of taking time to do it right.

He seemed to me much wiser then
Though we were only a year apart in age.
And it was so hard for me to understand
When Death wrote upon his page.

Well, it's been over twenty *anos* now
Since I've seen him face-to-face.
But the knife-like ache here in my heart,
Though dulled, is still in place.

But, now and then when the world closes in
And life's pressures grow too tight,
I can hear Fred whisper, "Just ease on in.
Take your time and do it right."

"Mil gracias, compadre."

Fred Eaves was my best friend from about the age of fourteen until his untimely death at the age of twenty-two. He was "cowboy to the bone," and I owe much of the cowboy skills that I have to him and to his family. He was a natural athlete and a great competitor. Fred was the Arizona High School Calf Roping Champ in 1962 and I have no doubt that he would have been a top PRCA roper had he lived. Fred was working for the Randall Ranches in 1966 in Maricopa, Arizona, when he was hit by a train and killed instantly. His death left a huge hole in my life and I think of Fred often. It has been well over thirty years and I miss his council and companionship still.

What's It All Mean?

(For Leon)

What's it all mean, when life's at this stage?
When you're now at the place that they call "middle age."
When fire of youth has fanned itself out,
And left you with gray hair and questions and doubt.

Dreams that once drove you have faded away;
They don't seem as important as they did yesterday.
You still wake at four-thirty, well before dawn,
But it's just force of habit; the "want to" is gone.

Bronc rides after breakfast that you craved as a lad
Are a thing of the past now, and damn, you're sure glad.
And that *potbellied viejo* who slowed down the crew
And grieved all the young hands has turned out to be you.

Yet you still crave it, the smell of burnt hair;
The bawl of *chicos* and *vacas* as you separate pairs.
The creak of the leather as you throw on your kack,
Or the feel of a good horse as he starts to untrack.

The long trot of a morning to scatter the hands;
The heeling and dragging and burning the brands.
Yes, you still love the life that you chose as a lad,
And you wouldn't take gold for the fun that you've had.

But somehow it's different as you look back over years
On dreams that have vanished, and it almost brings tears.
You always meant well were going to make it some day.
But the tracks that you made seem to have all blown away.

Leon Autrey
UL Ranch Mountainair, New Mexico

And sometimes you wish you could change the whole thing,
Produce once more the fever, the heat that youth brings.
And you know in your heart, you don't have to be told.
You're not afraid of dying; you're just scared of growing old.

I was visiting with my good friend, Leon Autrey, a while back and we got to discussing the problems tied to middle age. We finally decided that middle age is a bitch! To come to the realization that you just can't keep up with the youngsters anymore is a hard pill to swallow. We were both raised by dads who taught us to always make a "hand" no matter what the job was, and we have always tried to do just that. To accept the fact that you ain't a top hand anymore can make a feller grumpy.

I don't know about Leon, but, to keep people from thinking that I'm too old to be of any use at all, I have decided that the best thing to do in this situation is stand back, look wise, nod with approval or disapproval from time to time, and let them kids do the work. This would be sound advice if I could just make myself do it. But I can't seem to resist the chance to say, "Here, let me show you how to do that," or "Say, let me give you a hand there." Big mistake! Them damn kids can do it faster, better, and with no effort at all! I just hate 'em.

I tell you this for a fact. Middle age ain't for sissies or the faint of heart. You gotta be tough; and a taste for the flavor of "crow" ain't a bad thing to have either, 'cause you get to eat quite a bit of it.

The Lucky Man

The old cowboy's face was weathered and cracked,
And as brown as the skirts of his old Hamley kack.
His hands were all knurled and twisted and bent,
'Cause the brush had been thick in the places he'd went.

His ol' Stetson was stained from the hatband both ways,
And his old Olathe boots had seen better days.
His Blanchard's were shiny from good honest use,
And his ol' bottom lip held some good 'Hagen* snoose.

He said he'd been "housebroke" for quite a long time
And with "civilized" folks he got on right fine.
With them "up-town" folks he was now quite a hit;
He knew when not to swear and where not to spit.

Said he'd slowed down a lot from the days of his youth;
He had mellowed a bit, and was plumb full of couth.
He was honest and plain as an old block of salt,
And with long hard days he still found no fault.

To watch him work was a rare thing of beauty.
He gave good honest value, never shirked in his duty.
Horseback or afoot, he'd get the job done;
In truth, he was a workin' son-of-a-gun.

The young man from the city watched him in awe.
He could not understand all the things that he saw.
The old man was up every morning, long before dawn,
And he never slowed down till the daylight was gone.

*Hagen – short for Copenhagen snuff.

He had watched the old cowboy for several days,
Mystified by long hours and strange cowboy ways.
He thought, "This old man shouldn't be working for hire.
Surely he's old enough that he ought to retire."

He approached the old man and said, "Sir, I must say,
For a man of your age you work too hard these days.
You should give up this line and go have some fun.
Go lie on the beach, and soak up some sun.

"That's the reason I sweat in that office all day,
For the two weeks each year I come out and play.
You work all your life just to have a reward;
The chance to enjoy life's why we all work so hard."

The cowboy looked at the young man from the city,
And he smiled to himself as he thought, "What a pity."
He said, "Young man, set down, let's, you and me, talk.
You're wantin' to run when you ain't learned yet to walk.

"You say you work all year just for two weeks of fun.
If that there's the truth, let me say to you, son,
That the good Lord above said man should have joy,
And I think he meant for more than two weeks, my boy.

"Living life in the fast lane just ain't my style.
I try to savor each day, slow down, take a while.
Take each day as it comes, don't get in a hurry.
Enjoy all the small things, don't take time to worry.

"Each day's a new hand, so play the cards that you're dealt.
If it rains on you, OK, you ain't gonna melt.
It takes rain to make grass grow, same as the sun;
And you'll see more at a slow lope than you do at a run."
The young man was perplexed, he just couldn't see
How the ol' waddie could preach such a "fee-os-a-fee."
"Sir, I worked hard all year and saved lots of money
To spend a few days and see how this ranch was run.

"And it's worth every penny that I've spent on this trip,
And when I go home I'm going to leave a large tip.
So when you get the money, take my advice,
Spend some on yourself, go and buy something nice."

The old man said, "Son, it's plain you don't see,
Only a few workin' men are as lucky as me.
You paid good hard money to play on this spread
Then you gotta go back to a job that you dread.

"They pay me top wages to do every day
What you pay good money to come and call play.
Why, hell, son, it'd be foolish for me to retire
What I love best in the world, is what I do for hire."

I have been lucky enough to have made my living with and
around cowboys for most of my life. Now that I'm starting to get a
"little long in the tooth," I hope that I can pass along a little of the
"cowboy code" to the folks that I meet in my work and where I
perform.

The folks who live by "the code" are the salt of the earth, and I
thank God that I have been able to have known some of these
people and have been a small part of it all. I am indeed a "Lucky
Man."

All Out

The reporters gathered around the Champ
Right after the "last go."
Flash bulbs popped, and cameras clicked
'Cause he'd put on quite a show.

Tonight he had ridden the "unrideable;"
He'd scored a ninety-eight.
The crowd had got their money's worth
When he'd nodded for the gate.

"Is this the ride you'll want folks to remember
When you've hung up your gear?
To think of that almost *perfect score*
At the height of your career?"

The cowboy thought a moment,
And then he said, "I'll tell you, friend
How I'd like to be remembered
When this all comes to an end.

"I'd like it to be at Calgary,
Or maybe the Days of Cheyenne Frontier.
And for my draw in the final *go*
I'd want the Bucking Horse of the Year!

"I'd want to be so far in the lead
That when I made that ride,
All I'd have to do is "coast,"
And just get qualified.

"When I'd nod my head and they cracked the gate
That bronc would explode like TNT.
I'd start him good, and the battle'd begin,
And it's either him or me.

"Well, he'd buck like he'd never bucked before,
As though he were possessed.
And I would spur him jump for jump
With style and with finesse.

"Then just at the seven-second mark,
He'd squall and whirl around...
And to the astonishment of all the crowd,
He'd throw me to the ground.

"Well, I'd pick my Stetson off the ground
And hold it by the brim,
And as they led that ol' pony to the strippin' chute
I'd just 'tip' my hat to him."

Well, this answer was perplexing
To the reporters gathered round.
"You mean you'd want remembrance
For the day you got bucked down?"

The champ replied, "It ain't the bucking off that matters.
It's how you tried that counts.
I don't want to be remembered as one
Who just spurred hard on mediocre mounts.

"I want the young hands coming up
To know what rodeo and life are all about;
That what matters is how you play the game,
And that you've got to go *all out!*"

"All Out" is a poem that I wrote some years ago as a tribute to some of the tough hands that I've known, and especially to Larry Mahan. Larry and I were casual acquaintances back in the early sixties. We were both in high school, and it was long before anybody knew who he was. He had more "try and heart" than anyone I've ever been around. He drove an old beat-up Chevy truck and pulled a worn-out stock trailer behind it with a practice bronc in it. He never passed up an opportunity to practice. He knew what he wanted to do and he was willing to work for it.

The first year that Larry won the world title in bull riding, I saw him at a rodeo in El Cajon, California. He had drawn a bull there that, if he rode, he wasn't going to place on, and the ol' bull was "bad to hook." Most guys who were ahead in the standings at that point in the year would have "lifted the latch" and gone on to the next rodeo. Not Larry. He got on, made the ride, took a small hookin', and said. "That's rodeo."

As for this poem, I'm not sure that Larry would agree that this is how he would want to be remembered, but I've got a feeling that he might. He was a Champion's Champion, and dang sure one of my hero's.

 Take good care of your dreams, they belong to you!

Cosinero's Lament

Dawn's gray light filters through the wall
Of a tent somewhere in west New Mexico.
The old man turns the lantern off and pours a cup.
The boys headed out two hours ago.

The dishes are done, the Dutch ovens cleaned
And his other chores are through,
So he sits by the stove awhile and reminisces
While he sips his bitter brew.

Just listening to the boys this morning as they rode out,
Laughing, cussing, bragging like cowboys always do.
Familiar sounds, but this morning somehow melancholy;
Their cow camp camaraderie today has made him blue.

Ah, it must just be the changing weather,
Fall is in the air today for sure.
Got two more weeks in this damn cow camp,
Then four months of winter to endure.

But truth to tell, it ain't the weather
That's got him stretched out and tailed down.
It's remembering all the boys that he'd rode out with
And knowing he's the only one that's still around.

His mind's eye seeing round-up camps
Before his horseback days were through.
Memories of Ol' Buck and Dan and Constantine
And some other damn good buckaroos.

But Constantine went home to Old Mexico,
Way down by Sinaloa, someone said.
Dan's in a rest home out in Lubbock,
And for over fifteen years now Buck's been dead.

"Hell, these boys couldn't have carried our saddles,
Much less do the things we did.
The hands back then were all "Mucho Vaquero,"
These Jakes today are all just kids.

Why, we rode amongst the cedars boldly,
Expelling steer and wild cow brute.
None had been safe from our "reatas,"
We'd all been brushhands of repute.

And snorty, white-eyed, hump-backed horses?
Hell, that's how we warmed up each day.
We asked no succor of man nor boss
We'd earned a top hand's pay.

Why, I ought to make these boys a "sugar tit"
And get a teddy bear for each bed.
Replace their cold-backed horse herd
With a dude-broke pleasure string instead.

Ah, damn it, old man! You just got your back up
'Cause you envy them their youth.
You wish you could still brag and swagger,
You're just plain jealous, and that's the truth.

This getting old is sure a bitch;
Makes you feel cranky and kind'a mean.
To be around good young hands and watch 'em work,
I think it's plumb obscene.

But wait! Did I call them "good" young hands?
Yah, I did, and that's the unkindest cut of all.
To know they're just as good as we were
When we were young and riding tall.

So, I guess I'll just keep their coffee hot,
And make them pies and cakes for their sweet tooth.
But, I'm gonna bitch and gripe and cuss them,
Least they ever know the truth...

And that's that I'm proud to be amongst them,
And see in them the things we did.
And that I love the "little bastards,"
But, that last part I'll keep hid!

"Cosineros Lament" is a poem that I wrote while cooking in an elk camp for Drayton Martin several years ago. The guides and hunters had all gone one morning, and I was taking a few minutes to relax. The sun was just starting to come up and the "mood" was just right for a little melancholy thinkin'. Anyhow, the idea came to me that those old camp cooks must have had hundreds of mornings just like this, and I began to wonder what they thought about. I started the poem that morning, and had it about finished by the time we broke camp a week later.

A Cowboy Fairy Tale;

The True Story of Puss 'n' Boots, or, Now This Ain't No Crap

This tale I'm about to tell to you,
    ain't used to put kids down for a nap.
It's a sure enough cowboy story
    'cause folks, this ain't no crap!
I know you've heard a windy*
    told of how some cowboy roped a bear,
Or maybe twined a coyote
    bustin' through the prickly pear.

Heard tell how ol' Salty Jim
    roped a great big mountain lion;
Stretched him out and scorched his hide
    without even halfway tryin'.
Now, they can brag till Judgement Morn,
    But, boys, I'm here to say
That next to ropin' bobcats
    that stuff is mere child's play.

The morning that this tale began
    was clear and bright and warm.
Not a thing in sight to warn a feller
    of the impending storm.
I had ol' Boots in a short jig
    slippin' through the cedar trees,
When out of the brush steps a big bobcat
    just as casual as you please.

*Windy—a tall tale

He looked at me as if to say,
   "Well, cowboy, what are you doing here?"
He seemed to think this spot was his;
   he dang sure showed no fear.
Now, folks, this kind of impudence
   a buckaroo just can't tolerate,
Besides, I'd always wanted a bobcat skin.
   This musta been just fate.

See, I like to rope wild critters,
   and in the brush I ain't no faker.
I jerks my rope down and says,
   "Puss, get ready to meet your maker."
One swing and a throw was all it took
   and I had that feline caught
With a loop around his middle,
   while he spit and squalled and fought.

Boots turned and jerked ol' kitty off his feet
   and we lit out on the run.
Folks, I had roped myself a bobcat!
   Say, this was lots of fun.
I figured we'd drag him plumb to death,
   that'd do it quick and neat.
Ol' puss bouncing along behind,
   touchin' down about every thirty feet.

About now things went to hell,
   'cause of a fork in an ol' dead tree.
See, my slack got hung up there
   and that bode ill for Boots and me.
And physics ain't the kind of thing
   that this ol' boy was prone to study
When I was back in the schoolroom
   but, let me tell you, buddy,

If I had knowed just how p.o.-d
    a close-up bobcat looks,
You can damn well bet your bankroll
    I'd have opened up them books,
'Cause when that nylon twine
    was stretched as far as it would go,
That tree limb broke and here come my rope
    with that kitty-cat in tow.

Now, I was lucky 'cause that nylon rope
    didn't have enough trajectory
To catapult that turbulent tabby
    right up there on top of me.
But I guess my luck wasn't all that good
    now that I think back,
'Cause it did jerk ol' kitty
    right up there behind my kack.

Kitty's claws sunk into ol' Boot's butt
    like he was drillin' oil.
And that horse went heaven-bound
    like a spring that'd come uncoiled.
Now, as top-notch bronc rides go,
    this one must have been a sight.
A screamin' cowboy sharin' a ragin' bronc
    with a wildcat on the fight.

I swear, ol' Boots showed me tricks
    that I never thought he knew,
And he passed enough gas to get to Yuma
    as through the air we flew.
But *el gato* just set them meat hooks
    in Boot's butt a little deeper,
Then Boots kicks it into overdrive,
    and this hillside's gettin' steeper.

Now I'm a wild and woolly apparatus
    who can handle these conditions
But the look that feline was givin' me
    made me rethink my position.
Folks, I don't usually give up my saddle,
    but I decided to that day
'Cause ol' Puss was wantin' where I was,
    and I was in his way.

So I done the Apache love leap,
    got plumb familiar with a tree.
We embraced just like two sweethearts,
    entwined for all eternity.
Now, with me not there to help ol' Boots
    by sharin' in the fun,
He decided to quit his buckin',
    and just took off on the run.

If he'd been on the freeway,
    he'd a sure been hard to pass.
But, I guess it ain't that hard to hurry
    with a buzz saw on your ass.
'N' when you're mounted by a jockey
    wearin' fur and long sharp claws
Chances are you just don't give a damn
    about speed limit laws.

Now when Boots finally tops the ridge
    with ol' Puss still astraddle,
It occurs to me that that damn cat
    has just stole my horse and saddle.
I follow tracks for about two miles
    and I wind up in this draw
And there in the middle of the trail
    is a sight like I ain't never saw.

My rig is laying there intact,
    not a broken cinch nor strap nor rope.
Ol' Boots is gone and so is kitty,
    and I'm about to give up hope.
Then I heard Boots snort and whistle;
    he comes trottin' up to me,
Although he made a little detour
    'round a big old cedar tree.

He's a-blowin' snot and rollers
    and his eyes are showin' white.
I figure he's had all he wants
    of a bobcat on the fight.
The trip we made back to camp was interestin',
    to say the least;
Ol' Boots lookin' behind ever' rock
    for a spittin' furry beast.

Every bush seemed to hold a monster
    and every tree a ghost.
Shadows held his attention
    like a posthole holds a post.
Well, I had to turn ol'Boots out,
    He's just no good to me now,
He'll kick the door plumb off a stall
    if he hears someone say "meow."

You can't ride him past the tack room
    if he hears a house cat cough,
And just the smell of kitty litter
    will make him buck the bridle off.
And though I'm still the "ayatollah"
    of brush-poppers in these parts
I'm prone to be more careful
    just where I'm practicing my art.

And if I see a bobtailed feline
    whilst I'm trippin' down the slope,
I'll just let my eyes glaze over
    and forget I own a rope.
So I leave Boots home, and I don't rope cats.
    I now have new pursuits
Writin' poems and tellin' people
    about the real life "Puss 'n' Boots."

"Puss 'n' Boots" is a poem that I wrote just for the simple fun of it. I had heard an old story of a cowboy roping a bobcat, and jerking him up on the back of his horse and the ensuing wreck. Cowboys seem to have a natural gift for turning something that looks like it might be fun into a catastrophe, (pun definitely intended!). The interesting thing about writing this particular piece was that it seemed to take on a life of its own; I couldn't seem to find a stopping place. Finally, after consulting with Curt Brummett (master purveyor of cat information) and Sunny Hancock (He holds a "black belt" in the art of dumb cowboy stunts), I was finally able to bring the story to a somewhat logical end.

Kitty's claws sunk into Ol' Boots's butt like he was drillin' oil.

Order Form

❑ Yes! Please send me the following merchandise.

Name_____

Address_____

City_____ State_____ Zip_____

Phone_____Fax_____

Title	Qty.	Each	Total
Cowboy Poetry, Classic Rhymes by S. Omar Barker, Edited by Mason & Janice Coggin and Jon Richins. Winner of the Glyph Award and Finalist in the Academy of Western Artists 1999 Buck Ramsey Award for Best Poetry Book. Limited & Numbered Edition.	_____	$19.95	_____
Cowboy Poetry, Classic Rhymes by Henry Herbert Knibbs Compiled by Mason & Janice Coggin. Limited & Numbered Edition.	_____	$19.95	_____
Cowboy Poetry, Classic Rhymes by D. J. O'Malley Compiled from manuscript materials from Montana Historical Society Archives. Original photos. Edited by Mason & Janice Coggin. Limited & Numbered Edition.	_____	$30.00	_____
Cowboy Poetry, Contemporary Verse by Larry McWhorter. Edited by Janice & Mason Coggin.	_____	$19.95	_____

	Subtotal	_____
Arizona residents include 7% sales tax.	Tax	_____
Please add $3.50 for the first item, plus $1.00 for each additional item for shipping and handling.	S&H	_____
Foreign orders must be accompanied by a postal money order in U.S. funds.	**TOTAL**	_____

Send check or money order to: Cowboy Miner Productions
P.O. Box 9674, Phoenix, Arizona 85068
To order by phone call (602) 944-3763. Ask about quantity discounts.
Website: www.cowboyminer.com

Order Form

❑ Yes! Please send me the following merchandise.

Name_____

Address_____

City_____ State_____ Zip_____

Phone_____Fax_____

Title	Qty.	Each	Total
Cowboy Poetry, Rhymes, Reasons and Pack Saddle Proverbs by Chris Isaacs. Edited by Janice Coggin.	_____	$19.95	_____
Audio Tapes and CDs by Chris Issacs			_____
All Out and Other Poems (audio cassette)	_____	$10.00	_____
Chris Isaacs—Wanted, Needed, Tolerated! (audio cassette)	_____	$10.00	_____
Both Sides (audio cassette)	_____	$10.00	_____
Merry Christmas from Our Camp to Yours with Chris Isaacs, Buck Ramsey, Jean Prescott and Sky Shivers (audio cassette)	_____	$10.00	_____
Merry Christmas from Our Camp to Yours with Chris Isaacs, Budk Ramsey, Jean Prescott and Sky Shivers (CD)	_____	$15.00	_____
	Subtotal		_____
Please add $3.00 for the first item, plus $1.00 for each additional item for shipping and handling.	**S&H**		_____
Foreign orders must be accompanied by a postal money order in U.S. funds.	**TOTAL**		_____

Send check or money order to:
Chris Isaacs
P.O. Box 945, Eagar, AZ 85925

To order by phone call (520) 333-5800. Contact us about discounts.